SOUL BANQUETS

How Meals Become Mission in the Local Congregation

John Koenig

MOREHOUSE PUBLISHING
An imprint of Church Publishing Incorporated
Harrisburg—New York

Unless otherwise noted, the Scripture quotations contained herein are from the New Revised Standard Version Bible, copyright © 1989 by the Division of Christian Education of the National Council of Churches of Christ in the U.S.A. Used by permission. All rights reserved.

Morehouse Publishing, 4775 Linglestown Road, Harrisburg, PA 17105

Morehouse Publishing, 445 Fifth Avenue, New York, NY 10016

Morehouse Publishing is an imprint of Church Publishing Incorporated.

Cover design by Brenda Klinger

Library of Congress Cataloging-in-Publication Data

Koenig, John, 1938–
   Soul banquets : how meals become mission in the local congregation / John Koenig.
       p. cm.
   Includes bibliographical references.
   ISBN 978-0-8192-1926-8 (pbk.)
   1. Missions—Theory.   2. Dinners and dining—Religious aspects—Christianity.   3. Food—Religious aspects—Christianity.   4. Evangelistic work.   I. Title.
   BV2070.K64 2007
   253'.7—dc22
                                        2007009041

Printed in the United States of America

07 08 09 10 11 12   10 9 8 7 6 5 4 3 2 1

SOUL BANQUETS

How Meals Become Mission in the Local Congregation

To Elisabeth

Contents

Introduction

This is a book about the diverse meals of our community life as Christians, and about how God works through those meals to shape our ministries of outreach. To some readers, my quick reference up front to special acts of God in particular settings may seem overbold. After all, who of us would dare to claim certain knowledge of divine interventions? Even Paul, who writes at length about our experience of God's life in Christ, warns us that at present "we see in a mirror dimly" and know about celestial things only "in part" (1 Cor 13:12). On the other hand, Scripture also admonishes us to put words to our faith by giving an "account of the hope" that is in us (1 Pet 3:15). For me, this means writing about how my involvement with several outreach ministries over the years, interpreted by academic studies I've done of meals in the early church, has convinced me that we really can and should speak about mission-inspiring encounters with the Holy Trinity at our tables. Wow! As far as I can tell, however, most scholars and church leaders haven't focused much on this remarkable phenomenon. I hope the small volume I offer here will become a resource for helping us rediscover its power in our congregational life.

Supporting the views presented in this book is a solid consensus among students of the Bible today, from all points on the liberal-conservative spectrum, that meals have occupied a central place in Christian faith and practice from the very beginning. It's now common knowledge, for example, that Jesus loved to eat and drink and that in doing so he thought he was extending the welcome of God's

[handwritten annotations in margins: "food security in the NT world of believers?", "Plenitude -", "us", "The context of food, overeating, obesity, waste, greed, eating disorders", "Topic continue", "see exp.", "theme food norm to bodies"]

reign to all who dined with him, especially those on the margins of society. One of his most celebrated acts, the feeding of the five thousand, was understood by his followers to symbolize the presence of God's kingdom as a feast. It's the only miracle by Jesus recorded by all four canonical evangelists. Consistent with it is a famous declaration attributed to Jesus in the Fourth Gospel: "My food is to do the will of him who sent me and to complete his work" (4:34)—a mission statement if ever there was one. Actually, a large number of Jesus' sayings about the presence of God's reign in his ministry employ food imagery, and often enough they occur during conversations at table.[1] These special oracles reach their climax in an event that took place shortly before Jesus' death. At a last supper, hosted for his disciples on the evening of his arrest, he spoke astonishing words about his unique role in God's redemptive plan and, by implication, the role of those joining him that night (Mark 14:22–25). After the resurrection, Jesus' followers were quick to incorporate memories of this singular meal into their worship as they gathered each week to eat and drink together in house churches.

For the most part, we're already familiar with these traditions. What we haven't recognized clearly enough, I think, is how the major New Testament writers show early believers enthusiastically adopting Jesus' position on the connection between meals and mission. In fact, I think that virtually all gatherings for food and drink in the first century churches, particularly those evolving into what we now call the Eucharist, were catalysts for missionary activity. That is, they stimulated an outreach by believers, in word and deed, not only to people unfamiliar with Jesus' ministry but also to those unconvinced by his claims.

One distinctive feature of the earliest mission-meal connection that's emerged repeatedly from my biblical studies is a fervent expectation among believers that the Holy Spirit would be present in their eating and drinking to confer gifts for ministry. Indeed, it looks as if meals very quickly became the primary settings in New Testament communities for the naming, receiving, and practice of spiritual gifts. For example, there's strong evidence to support the view that prophets, teachers, and healers all took up their Spirit-led vocations most regularly during worship at table (See 1 Cor 11–12). This finding alone has reinforced my conviction that our missionary outreach today can profit enormously from a focused exploration of what typically occurred at the meals described in the New Testament and other Christian literature of the first century.

In two previous books I've ventured a few observations on the degree to which we can appropriate these ancient experiences as our own, while maintaining our integrity as twenty-first century Christians.[2] Until now, however, I've not had the chance to talk over my views or test their validity in a systematic way with contemporary church leaders. This project has finally given me that opportunity. In the following chapters I'm pleased to share the results of some fifty interviews I've conducted with lay and ordained people from many denominations, most of them actively engaged in congregational ministries where meals figure prominently. Usually we talked over cups of coffee or at lunches.

The interviews have yielded a rich collection of stories about meals in church life today, plus a host of reflections on their missionary potential that may be richer still. When I present this material in the chapters that follow, I frequently weave it together with the results of my biblical studies. My hope is that readers will find this mixture rising to the level of a dialogue in which old and new things illumine one another, producing fresh insights and empowerings for our common life. Nearly all the people I interviewed, and I myself, felt that this was in fact happening as we talked. But we are clearly a biased sample! Readers will naturally draw their own conclusions—perhaps while fortifying themselves with a little food and drink. Meal settings would be particularly appropriate, I think, for groups discussing the book in churches or in the homes of members.

For a number of reasons I've chosen to call my volume *Soul Banquets*. First, this phrase makes the point that at meals where we're able to discern God's presence, something happens to us in our deepest selves. Our very being and purpose for existence are addressed—sometimes with a nurturing force that seems to come from heaven itself (Ignatius of Antioch called the Eucharist "the medicine of immortality"), sometimes with a challenge to undertake new tasks that both frighten and attract us because we sense that we have been created for them (Eph 2:10). On more than a few occasions, the nurture and the challenge come wrapped up in each other.

Second, the word "banquet" in our title implies that the meals we'll be looking at manifest a divine abundance (as in the feeding of the five thousand) and a celebration of goodness that belongs to us as well as to God. This conjunction of abundance and celebration can reveal itself in all manner of meal settings, from elaborate feasts to simple sharings of tea and cookies. In fact, the quantity of our table fare proves finally irrelevant. Similarly, while high-quality food is always desirable, because it begets praise for God's created order, it can't always be found and isn't necessary. Furthermore, the goodness we savor at these meals often emerges from the most trying circumstances, when sadness, tragedy, and deprivation seem to be in control. These meals too we can call banquets, because in them God co-opts every evil power through the cross of Christ.

Third, and by no means least, the phrase *Soul Banquets* is meant as a tribute to the meal practices of African-American churches. Although most racial and ethnic groups have a feeling for what "soul food" is, this precise and profound way of naming it comes most directly from the hard lives of black people in North America. For many of them, the lunches and suppers and picnics of congregational life provided a deep feeding that couldn't be found elsewhere. In several areas of the United States today this is still the case. And of course when people use the term "soul food," they aren't just talking about an inner feeding. They mean real food, scrumptious food prepared by loving hands from local produce—and lots of it. To this day, a number of black churches host great meals right after the Sunday service that are understood to be a continuation of the worship. In effect, they bless the congregation's transition back into the everyday world, consecrating souls and bodies alike for the work of the Lord. Readers will find that several of the meal ministries reported on in the following chapters derive from, or approximate, this African-American practice.

In the book's subtitle, there's a single word I'd like to expand on: the ubiquitous term "mission." These days, nearly all Christians talk and write a lot about mission, agreeing that it's a good thing for the church—or it *is* the church in action. A few critics have pointed out that since the word "mission" turns up so often in our everyday rhetoric (one thinks of military or corporate "mission statements"), it can easily lose its original New Testament meaning of being sent out by God or Jesus. (See, for example, Matt 19:5–16; 28:18–20; John 17:17–18; Acts 26:14–18). I'm sure that's a real danger, but even so we dare not give up on the term because it's so basic to our Christian self-understanding. Moreover, as Brian McLaren notes, it's one of the few big concepts that still provide common ground for the various liberal and conservative branches of the church.[3] While the former tend to see outreach ministry primarily in terms of our transforming the world's social, political, and economic structures, and the latter give priority to our telling the good news of Jesus, both groups generally admit that a comprehensive understanding of mission in the Bible includes all these activities.

In *A Generous Orthodoxy,* McLaren furnishes a diagram for clarifying our Christian mission that makes use of three circles and several arrows. The largest of the circles stands for the world. Inside it is a smaller one, located off to the side so that it doesn't occupy the same center point as the world circle. It stands for the church. Inside this we find a third circle, again off to the side, which represents me and my concerns. What we notice right away is that "I" am not the center of the world or the church; and the church, in turn, is not the center of the world. From the "me" circle arrows extend outward toward church and world. Likewise, from the circle of the church arrows point in the direction of the world. Although he doesn't spell it out explicitly, McLaren assumes—correctly, I think—that God inhabits all three circles and crafts the arrows, with our willing cooperation. Naturally this symbolism has its limits. Some would argue that the church does in fact reside at the center of the world. But that's a topic for another book.

I like the way McLaren moves from his diagram to a fuller discussion of what he calls "missional Christian faith." He states that the approach he's recently come to adopt

> eliminates old dichotomies like "evangelism" and "social action." Both are integrated in expressing [God's] saving love for the world. Those who want to become Christians (whether through our proclamation or demonstration) we welcome. Those who don't, we love and serve, joining God in seeking their good, their blessing, their shalom. This approach gets rid of distinctions like *ministry* (what we do in the church) and

mission (what we do outside of it) since ministry is for mission from the start.[4]

[handwritten marginalia: receive & share Charism / Grace]

Later on, McLaren summarizes the matter this way: "My mission isn't to figure out who is already blessed, or not blessed or unblessable. My calling is to be blessed so that I can bless everyone."[5] In the following pages I'll try to show that growing into this kind of missional perspective, properly tempered by humility, has much to do with living out our roles as guests and hosts at the meals of the church.

There's one more angle on mission that we ought to consider here. It has to do with the realization that our own outreach efforts are at best responses to and participations in a plan of God for the world's redemption much larger and grander than we can imagine (Eph 3:20). We don't begin by creating our own mission, either locally or nationally; we hear it first as a calling to follow, to join up with a procession led by Jesus and the saints that's already under way. Shortly after World War II a number of theologians associated with the newly formed World Council of Churches began using the Latin term *Missio Dei* (literally: "the mission of God") to describe this divine initiative in our outreach ministries. No one has written more lucidly about the term than South African missiologist David Bosch, who died too young in 1992 as the result of an auto accident. According to Bosch:

> We have to distinguish between *mission* (singular) and *missions* (plural). The first refers primarily to the *Missio Dei* (God's mission), that is, God's self-revelation as the One who loves the world, God's involvement in and with the world, the nature and activity of God, which embraces both the church and the world, and in which the church is privileged to participate. *Misso Dei* enunciates the good news that God is a God-for-people. *Missions* (. . . the missionary ventures of the church), refer to particular forms, related to specific times, places, or needs, or participation in the *Missio Dei*.[6]

Bosch's thoughts will feed directly into our exploration of meals as opportune times for the defining and empowering of our outreach ministries. In fact, the term *Missio Dei* will turn up frequently in our biblical studies and interview results.

That's especially so in the last chapter of this book where we begin to look at how God's end-time feast "for all peoples" (Isa 25:6) not only affirms a traditional Christian understanding of sacred meals but also pushes us beyond it. Here a major question becomes: What might God be doing in the huge number of table settings today where Christians and non-Christians dine together? A related question, even more difficult for most church members, I think, concerns how we might see God at work in the table rituals of religions that we find strange or offensive. In response to these challenges, we'll suggest a few new guidelines for etiquette at our soul banquets today, taking the view that God's mission tends to surprise us when we're eating and drinking out there on the frontiers of our comfort zones.

Over the past three years many people have helped me bring this volume to birth. A sabbatical leave, offered to me by the General Seminary Board of Trustees for the fall semester of 2005, proved absolutely essential to my work. So did a generous grant from the Conant Fund for teachers at Episcopal seminaries that allowed me to travel and host the church leaders I interviewed at meals—though sometimes they insisted on providing all the hospitality themselves. Here I particularly want to thank the Rev. Bud Holland, Director of the Office for Ministry Development of the Episcopal Church, and his staff associates, the Rev. Lynne Grifo and Ms. Molly Shaw. Together they shepherded a committee process that caused the actual grant check to appear in my mailbox.

Among the many leaders I had the privilege of interviewing, two deserve special expressions of gratitude. The Very Rev. Dr. Robert Giannini, who recently became Dean Emeritus of Christ Church Cathedral, Indianapolis and President Emeritus of our Board at General, not only welcomed me most warmly to his busy congregation, enduring a barrage of my questions about meals and mission, but also provided names of several other interviewees in the Indianapolis area. Some of the richest material in this book came from these contacts. In Berkeley, California the Rev. C. Robbins Clark ("Robbin" to those who know her best) serves as Rector of St. Mark's Episcopal Church. I've delighted in conversations with Robbin for almost eight years now, many of them on the topic of meals and mission. Not only is she known as a highly competent rector and excellent preacher; she's also a superb cook, who believes that church gatherings in her home for meals are foundational to her ministry. I think she's right! Her wisdom graces many of the pages of this book.

Mr. Richard Service, recently a student at the General Seminary, provided much help as an editorial assistant and honest critic during the final stages of the book's production. I couldn't have finished the writing without his expertise. My wife, Elisabeth, with whom I share daily bread and many exotic dishes, mostly of her invention, has given me steady encouragement. I always think of her first whenever I put the words "soul" and "banquet" together, and so this book is dedicated to her. Finally, I want to mention three food-related friendships that have evolved over the course of the last fifty years—in one case sixty years. Here I'm referring to classmates from my school days in Indiana: Richard Ford, Graden Walter, and Bill Wimberly, with whom I graduated from Wabash High in 1956. Somehow the four of us have managed to keep on meeting face to face, often at their initiative and nearly always over food and drink. I owe these friends a lot and rejoice at the prospect of our deepening communion as we continue our journeys toward the Heavenly Banquet. Finally, I offer my deep gratitude to Morehouse Executive Editor Nancy Fitzgerald, who has guided this book to its completion with many words of encouragement. Readers won't be surprised to learn that she and I celebrated the final, final version of the manuscript with a New York deli breakfast.

In each relationship I've mentioned above a key element has been table talk that gets beyond pleasantries. Looking back, I'd say that nearly always some kind of revelation was taking place. So I know at least something of what the psalmist means when he writes: "Taste and see that the Lord is good" (Ps 34:8). In the following pages I try to encourage us all not only to savor that goodness, repeatedly and at length, but also to share it lavishly so that it multiplies.

John Koenig
Chelsea Square
Eastertide, 2007

CHAPTER ONE

The Mission-Meal Synergy

The shrimp salad at Michael's Restaurant was superb, and we couldn't help praising it as we dug into our over-generous portions. But our table talk quickly turned to other matters. My lunch partner, the Rev. Lyndon Harris, was about to complete his assignment as priest in charge at St. Paul's Chapel, the small eighteenth-century church in lower Manhattan that had miraculously survived the destruction of the World Trade Center towers across the street. Survival alone had granted the church a certain iconic status in the days immediately following 9/11, but St. Paul's did not rest on that reputation. Only a week or so after the attacks, the congregation's mission of hospitality to the crowds of emergency workers at Ground Zero became legendary. Having served as a night chaplain at the church some months later, I knew about its diverse ministries first hand, but I wanted to learn more about how they came into being, especially those that involved meals. So I asked Lyndon for an hour of his time, suggesting that we talk over lunch. He responded graciously, with the proviso that we had to eat at Michael's. I soon found out why.

Lyndon explained that this restaurant, about two hundred yards from the World Trade Center complex, was a favorite haunt for church staffers even prior to 9/11. No loud music deafened its customers, and because it was located below street level cell phones didn't work there. Wonder of wonders, actual conversations at table became the norm. After 9/ll, when choking white dust filled the air for days, Michael's functioned as a kind of bunker, continuing to operate when other area restaurants were forced to shut down.

1

But there was much more to it than that, Lyndon said. As he and his co-workers at St. Paul's gathered around the table, several times a day during that first awful week, they felt that their praying and planning came naturally, in fact, became one and the same thing. Old hierarchies and interpersonal tensions seemed to melt away as the companions sensed that they were being guided by a greater Power. Chaos reigned outside, but here a kind of inner peace sustained them. The many New Testament stories of Jesus' words and actions at table came quickly to mind, leading the group to resolve that their very first congregational response to the situation must be to provide round-the-clock food and drink for the firefighters, police, National Guard soldiers, and rescue/retrieval workers of all sorts who were crowding into lower Manhattan.

At first, the meals were simple. No one could enter the church building until engineers had established that it was structurally sound. But the delay didn't prevent congregational workers (along with many volunteers who had no formal relationship with the church) from setting up grills on the street to serve burgers and soft drinks. Very quickly this operation moved to the large front porch of the church, which was found to be safe. A small crisis occurred when city health officials ruled that all outside cooking had to cease because of the poor air quality. But almost simultaneously other officials gave the go-ahead to enter the sanctuary. The bottom line was that a moveable feast had come into being, a non-stop provision of food and drink that continued for well over a year.

Soon after the meal service at St. Paul's began, Lyndon and his co-workers made an important decision about its character. Precisely in the midst of this tragic setting, they reasoned, the food and drink they were furnishing ought to be of the highest possible quality. As Lyndon put it: "We wanted people to see and savor the extravagance of Christ's love." Almost from the beginning a restaurant owner in the area, Martin Cowart, became the operation's "food captain" and began to enlist the help of his professional friends. Basic provisions and fully cooked meals poured in on a regular basis, some of them from world-renowned restaurants. Lyndon recalled being blown away one night when a large delivery of chicken dinners arrived from the Waldorf Astoria.

TABLE FELLOWSHIP — Powerful picture at 9/11 brought people together who don't often sit with each other

PIT FELLOWSHIP) Disaster + food

Ten days after 9/11, when the church building was fully secured, public celebrations of the Eucharist began to take place every noon. The timing was intentional. People who came to lunch could also attend the service, and while the majority of diners did not join the worship in a direct way, they honored this special offering as a sign of their host's distinctive mission. Without conflict, the wall between "secular" and "sacred" virtually disappeared. Everyday talk continued at food stations in the back of the church even as the liturgy proceeded up front around the altar. Yet none of the worshipers complained about irreverence on the part of "non-participants," nor did people milling around the lunch tables protest that religion was being forced upon them.

A volunteer chaplain from New Jersey described his experience of St. Paul's this way:

> I attended mass with the most incredible hodgepodge of humanity I've ever seen gathered in a church. . . . There were the chiropractors and massage therapists doing their thing along the side aisles. There were rescue workers sleeping or eating lunch—some of them Jews wearing yarmulkes under their fire helmets. There were National Guard troops from the farms and forests of upstate New York looking very young and lost in the big city. People sat on the floor and on the steps leading to the choir loft. Some of the rescue workers who had not shown much interest in the mass when it began found themselves drawn into the ancient prayers that promise life forever with God and ended up taking communion with tears in their eyes. This was Christ's church in all its messiness, diversity, ambiguity, brokenness, and holiness. And it was truly beautiful.[1]

Somehow the emergency feeding program and the ritual meals at St. Paul's were beginning to flow together, reinforcing and enriching each other as facets of God's mysterious welcome.

Meals and Mission

I've chosen the Greek term "synergy" to describe this complex set of interactions. The word comes from *syn* ("with") and *ergon* ("work"), but it means more than "cooperation." Webster defines it as "cooperative action of discrete agencies such that the total effect is greater than the sum of the two effects taken independently." Synergy is also a good biblical word, since a verbal form of it appears in Romans 8:28, the famous passage in which Paul declares that "all things work together (*synergei*) for good for those who love God." Some scholars think that the real subject of this verse is not "all things" but the Holy Spirit, who in 8:27 is said to be interceding "for the saints according to the will of God." If that's true, the proper reading for 8:28 would be: "We know that [the Spirit] causes all things to work together for good. . . ." Because we'll have a lot to say throughout this book about the work of the Holy Spirit in the Eucharist and other church-related meals, we'll want to keep this alternative reading in mind.

We might be going too far if we claimed that the resonance between the two kinds of meals at St. Paul's—those in the back and those at the altar—*created* the plethora of ministries to recovery workers, but everyone who visited felt the force of that resonance. One can make a strong case that people who just "showed up" at St. Paul's with new ideas and talents for service did so to a large degree because they understood that this survivor church had made a long-term commitment to nurturing meals that defied easy distinctions between the physical and the spiritual. The chiropractors and podiatrists, the psychologists and musicians, the volunteers dispensing gloves and clean socks and aspirins to workers in the dreadful Pit—these were not necessarily people of deep faith, or any faith at all in the traditional sense. But most of them discerned a mystery at work in the table fellowship at St. Paul's, a sacred task in which they wanted to participate.

Of course one could argue that the situation at Ground Zero was so unique that it alone produced the special mission-meal synergy evident at St. Paul's, but I think that just the opposite is true. I've come to believe that what happened at this small church in lower Manhattan is a window into what could happen (and often happens already) in all our congregations—whether we are large or small, whether or not we find ourselves in crisis situations, whether or not feeding programs occupy a major place in our outreach ministries. If we don't experience a mission-meal synergy in our churches at present, or we discover it only on rare occasions, we can take steps to open ourselves more fully to its ongoing presence and power. All of us, I am guessing, want the outreach ministries of our churches to be more effective than they are, but we often don't know quite how to concentrate our efforts to make this happen. My reading of Scripture and my interviews over the past few years with leaders in a number of North American churches suggest that a very good place to begin is with an assessment of the diverse meal events that occur right now in and around the lives of our congregations.

Encouragement from the Bible

Scripture itself practically mandates this kind of assessment. The Old Testament abounds in stories about meals, many of which serve to reveal God's presence and deeper purposes for the whole world. Of these, perhaps the best known concerns the patriarch Abraham's welcoming of three strangers who approach his Bedouin tent at high noon. The travelers, who are simply called "men," have variously been identified as prophetic messengers, angels, or in the case of the Orthodox church tradition, the persons of the Holy Trinity. Nothing in the text of Genesis 18, where the story is recorded, indicates that Abraham knows who the three are, yet he and Sarah prepare a lavish feast for them. This probably means that we should think of the ancient couple as demonstrating a special talent or virtue for welcoming the stranger. Indeed, in later Jewish writings Abraham comes to be known as the patron saint of hospitality.[2] The real climax of the story occurs when one of the guests, apparently still feasting, suddenly announces: "I will surely return to you in due season, and . . . Sarah shall have a son" (18:10). Hearing this, Sarah, who is more than ninety years old, laughs to herself in disbelief and is immediately called to account by the speaker, who seems to be reading her mind. Abraham is not reprimanded here, but we already know from previous stories in Genesis that he, too, has essentially given up on the promise God made to him at the time of his calling that his own natural descendants would become a great nation (12:3, 10–20; 16:1–6; 17:15–22). Contrary to all expectations, this mealtime prophecy somehow moves the plan of God forward, and by Genesis 21, Abraham and Sarah's son Isaac has been born.

Without stretching the Genesis narrative too far, we can think of this meal in missionary terms. Abraham is the very embodiment of "outreach ministry." He welcomes the strangers enthusiastically, running from his tent to greet them with a low bow and then urging them to rest under a nearby tree while the meal is being prepared. He sets food and drink before them, far more generously than the law of desert hospitality requires, while he stands by as a servant. Then, in the course of the meal itself, another kind of mission comes to light, for Abraham and Sarah hear a divine word that challenges their despair. They are strengthened for their greater mission—to persist in their journey until they become progenitors of God's chosen people Israel, through whom, in turn, all the families of the earth will be blessed (Gen 12:1–3). Here, during a guest-meal by the Oaks of Mamre (Gen 18:1), the *Missio Dei* for all humanity is revealed once again, and two chosen figures find new courage to play their unique roles within it.

Much later, when Abraham's descendants have in fact become a people, the biblical record shows that two distinctive meal celebrations emerge from the nation's common life to express its covenant relationship with God. These rituals are the weekly Sabbath eve supper, along with meals on the day of the Sabbath, and the yearly Passover Seder, or order of worship at table. Nothing explicit is said about Sabbath meals in the Old Testament, but there may be an allusion to them in Exodus 16:22–30, where the people of Israel are commanded to gather twice as much manna on the sixth day of the week and bake or boil as much as they want so as to make it last through the next day, on which they are to rest. In any case, meals on the Sabbath became a fixture of Israel's identity sometime during the Second Temple Period (roughly 450 BCE–70 CE), well before the time of Jesus. The yearly Passover festival, culminating in a dramatic communal meal, is well attested in both the Old and New Testaments. The foundational story occurs in Exodus 12. By the first century, Passover had come to commemorate not only Israel's flight from Egypt and deliverance at the Red Sea, but also its wilderness wanderings. In addition, the festival stirred up a fervent hope for Israel's political and spiritual restoration. All of these themes appear in contemporary Passover celebrations.

The Sabbath and Passover meals are best understood as community-defining activities rather than attempts to include non-Israelites.

On the other hand, there's evidence of Jews living in cities outside Palestine at the time of Jesus who interacted with their Gentile neighbors in ways that allowed them some degree of participation in synagogue worship. Whether this openness also applied to meal celebrations in Jewish homes is uncertain but not impossible, especially in the case of Gentiles sympathetic to Judaism.[3] Jews who welcomed Gentiles most intentionally may have done so to fulfill God's promise that through Abraham and Sarah's descendants, all of the world's nations would be blessed. (See the inclusive interpretations of Sabbath-keeping in Isaiah 56:1–8 and 58:12–14.)

Nearly all contemporary scholars agree that in the synoptic gospels of the New Testament (Matthew, Mark, and Luke) Jesus' personal meal practices stand out as radically hospitable. Contrary to the customs of his day, which required one's dining partners to be morally upright and ritually clean, he regularly ate with tax collectors and sinners. Even when Jesus appeared to be setting up boundaries by inviting a small group of his disciples to a last supper on the night of his arrest, he intended not to exclude people but rather to draw those who had accompanied him to Jerusalem (probably women as well as men)[4] more deeply into his expansive mission for the world, which he foresaw as continuing after his death. Well before the origin of our Christian Eucharist, Jesus used a meal setting to inspire a vocation for outreach in his followers.[5]

Some New Testament stories of Jesus' post-resurrection appearances also reveal a mission-meal synergy. For example, in the story of the two disciples on the road to Emmaus who come to recognize the Risen One at their dinner table when he blesses and breaks bread, Luke hastens to add that the two immediately speak of their encounter as a conversion from despair to hope. As they do so, they decide against continuing their journey to Emmaus and instead hurry back to Jerusalem to share their experience with the other disciples, who just happen to be dining themselves. Once again, Jesus appears, eats a bit of fish to prove that he still inhabits a human body, and then announces that

> repentance and forgiveness of sins is to be proclaimed in [my] name to all nations, beginning from Jerusalem. You are witnesses

of these things. And see I am sending upon you what my Father promised; so stay here in the city until you have been clothed with power from on high (Lk 24:47–49).

Virtually all commentators understand the "power from on high" to be the Holy Spirit. With Jesus' prophetic promise, an ordinary meal becomes a commissioning ceremony.

Once the predicted coming of the Holy Spirit has occurred at Pentecost, the earliest disciples discover that their daily community meals have begun to function as missionary events with unique opportunities for spreading the gospel. In Acts, Luke tells us that the Spirit-filled believers "devoted themselves to the apostles' teaching and fellowship, to the breaking of bread and the prayers" (Acts 2:42). But these meetings were not secret enclaves. Although the meals took place in the homes of disciples, they were public enough to be noticed by non-disciples and proved attractive to some. Luke reports that believers "ate their food with glad and generous hearts, praising God and having the good will of all the people [in Jerusalem]. And day by day, the Lord added to their number those who were being saved" (Acts 2:46–47).

Methodist bishop Mortimer Arias has nicely termed this flow of events "centripetal evangelism," implying that "outsiders" felt themselves drawn into the community of Jesus' disciples by their words and practices, especially during celebrations at table.[6] The most natural reading of Acts 2:46–47, is that it presupposes interactive contact between believers and their neighbors at church meals.[7] There joyful worship, wonders and signs, testimonies, teachings, and a radical sharing of goods with the poor (Acts 2:43–45) apparently combined to produce requests for baptism. Although we would dearly love to know whether baptism always preceded participation in these earliest church meals, the text does not tell us. Probably we should imagine an inconsistency of practice since full "sacramental" understandings were only beginning to emerge.

In a book describing the religious experience of the New Testament believers in Jesus, Luke Timothy Johnson highlights the importance of divine-human encounters at table by entitling one of his chapters "Meals Are Where the Magic Is."[8] I like Johnson's title but want to add that quite often the New Testament presses us to modify it just a bit so that it becomes: "Meals Are Where the Missionary Magic Is." Of course this emphasis on mission at the table doesn't mean that every meal associated with our congregational life must yield a payload of conversions in order to be "biblical." Surely Jesus' first followers often needed just to enjoy themselves at table, with no conscious agendas. And so do we. But the richness of the biblical stories about meals—which we have only begun to explore—strongly encourages us to look at the whole range of our own meals more prayerfully, reflecting on the ways our participation in them enhances our church's mission activity. Or doesn't.

My guess—in fact my conviction—is that we have seriously under-valued our church meals, both ritual and informal, as opportunities for missionary discernment, planning, and outreach. The people of St. Paul's discovered at Ground Zero that some meals prepared them for mission, and some meals literally *became* mission. Often they were capable of doing both. But for us to realize this potential in our congregations, we, like the disciples on the road to Emmaus, must have our eyes opened by the transforming presence of Christ at our tables. It is this presence, the apostle Paul tells us in his long discourse on the Lord's Supper (1 Cor 12–14), that enables us to recognize and claim our distinctive gifts for ministry, following them into works of love that will accomplish "far more than all we can ask or imagine" (Eph 3:16–20).

Meals Abounding

Where do we start in our own congregations? For most of us, it won't be hard to write up a quick list of church-sponsored meal events where boundaries between members and non-members, insiders and outsiders are often crossed. Some readers will think right away of the feeding programs and food pantries that they administer for needy people in their neighborhoods. Close to the top of our lists, I suspect, will be coffee hours after the main Sunday service. Here old-timers and more recent members can mingle, and both groups can present themselves as hosts to visitors. Some congregations have discovered that coffee hours can even be times when insiders and visitors alike find it natural to talk together about what has just happened in worship, particularly as it relates to the church's mission.

At Trinity English Lutheran Church in downtown Fort Wayne, Indiana, one highlight of the church year is the Septemberfest, a giant picnic-like event that takes place on a farm not far from the city. Informal worship is scheduled at a time close to the main meal. Senior pastor Frederick Hasecke reports that for many people the most enjoyable features of the event have to do with its intergenerational character—lots of children and old people come—and an atmosphere of freedom in which old members, new members, and prospective members mingle easily.

A rather different tradition of eating and drinking together has developed at an Episcopal church I know in southern California. Some years ago a group of men came to the rector proposing a dinner club for members that they wanted to call "Eat, Drink, and Be Merry." Recognizing the ironic reference to 1 Cor 15:32 and fearing that an exclusive in-group was being formed, the rector found himself unenthused about this idea. Taking a chance, however, he gave his blessing to the club, took part in it himself, and was surprised when group leaders automatically reached out to their unchurched friends. Within the first year, five new families had joined the church after initially affiliating with the club.

With a little more reflection we can enlarge our list of boundary-crossing meals to classes for inquirers where food is served (the Alpha Program is one version of this), various congregational dinners that are open to visitors, AA groups, prayer breakfasts, and Bible studies with snacks, all of which potentially create holy space for the welcoming of strangers. We can also add business lunches that involve members of the congregation and meal sharing social action groups where church people mix easily with the general public. Even meal events that seem to be mostly in-house, like small-group agape meals or religious book discussions over dessert and coffee, tend to attract non-member spouses and curious visitors. Some readers (rightly, I think) will call to mind as well those numerous pastoral visitations where clergy or lay ministers share food with hospital patients and homebound people who are not necessarily members of the congregation. Jesus said: "Where two or three are gathered in my name, I am there among them" (Matt 18:20), and a good case can be made that this promise was heard by Matthew's readers as echoing an early rabbinic saying about the presence of God at meals.[9,10]

Many congregations develop specialty meals that reflect both the character of their community life and their distinctive outreach activities. I know of a church on the West Coast that regularly provides musical offerings of high quality to the public, often in the evenings. Typically these are followed by what the church calls "festive receptions" where all sorts and conditions of humanity mix in the parish hall. A large Lutheran congregation in the upper Midwest is famous for its annual Sportsmen's Dinner at which young athletes of many religious persuasions (or none) are honored. Catholic churches, especially in the Southwest, are known for celebrating outdoor fiestas in the Spanish tradition that are always open to the community surrounding the church. The new Cathedral of Our Lady of the Angels in Los Angeles is built on a huge plaza that practically begs for such festivities. In Chicago's West Loop, Old St. Patrick's Church invites its neighborhood to what it calls the "World's Largest Block Party," an annual affair that features internationally known rock, jazz, and swing bands, as well as plenty of food.[11]

Some congregations sponsor coffee houses in commercial districts to meet unchurched neighbors on their own turf. Some push the envelope even further. Craig Blomberg reports that in Auckland, New Zealand, "two Christian men . . . rented a nightclub, set up what they called 'Parallel Universe', and produced multiscreen, multimedia presentations with a thoughtfully contexualized gospel message while patrons ate, drank, and socialized."[12] A variation on this approach is the "Theology on Tap" movement that is growing among U.S. churches. *New York Times* reporter Katie Zezima describes one local version of the program as follows:

Manchester, N.H., Nov. 10, 2005—On Thursday night, the Rev. Marc Montminy's pulpit was a cocktail table, and his flock all had their I.D.'s checked by a burly bouncer at the door. . . . Father Montminy was speaking to the Roman Catholic Diocese of Manchester's Theology on Tap program, a series of lecture and question-and-answer sessions held in bars that engage

young adults in discussion about Catholic doctrine. . . . The
goal, organizers said, is to explain and discuss the church's view
on topics of faith and social issues, and to dispel any precon-
ceived notions. A drink in a familiar place usually helps loosen
up young people reluctant to inquire about touchy topics, organizers said.[13]

This event and all the others I've described presuppose some kind
of missionary intentionality on the part of those who sponsor them.
Indeed, it seems that when churches are doing their job, the good news
of the gospel is regularly shared at table with people whose names are
not found on congregational membership rolls.

Theoretically, the same kind of thing happens at the ritual meal on
Sundays that marks us most distinctively as Christians: our Eucharist,
or Lord's Supper. But here things get complicated since our various
denominations often part company over issues of open or closed communion, frequency of celebration, literal or symbolic interpretations
of the bread and wine, and the like. As far as mission is concerned, this
lack of unanimity sends a bad message, and we sometimes compound
it in our local churches when we fail to integrate our ritual meals with
the other meals of our congregational life. Part of the problem may
stem from the fact that the Holy Communion portion of our church
services is not usually experienced as a real meal. In fact, some of our
service-oriented meals outside the sanctuary can feel more sacramental than our formal Sunday liturgies.[14] My hope is that by working
through the issues raised in this book we can learn to see and claim
the deep connections, renewed each day by the risen Christ, between
his unique Table and all the other tables we set as his servants. This
connection actually happened at St. Paul's, Ground Zero, and I believe
it can happen in our own congregations as well. If it does, both our
callings to mission and our abilities to fulfill them may well take a
quantum leap forward.

Soul Banquets

I like the phrase "soul banquets" because it helps us to stay focused
on the transcendent dimensions of our meals. What I *don't* want to

suggest by it is that the meals we'll be looking at in the following pages affect only, or mainly, our inner lives—our souls as opposed to our bodies. Here I take my cue from members of black churches in North America who love to talk about soul food. And of course they mean *real* chicken and collard greens, with all the fixings. Still, my friends tell me that what ultimately makes something food for the soul is its ability to satisfy both the inner and outer person at the same time. Some would even insist that it reunites our bodies and souls when they are out of sync.

Almost all of us know what this means. We remember special dishes and drinks and gatherings at table that have bound up the loose ends of our lives and in some cases continue to do so. We laugh at Garrison Keillor's encomia to tuna casseroles, but we know what he's getting at. Sometimes "Holy Communion" is the best term we can come up with to describe our most memorable meals: communion with the universe, with our neighbors and families and enemies, communion with our deeper selves as physical/spiritual unities. Often we idealize these moments, but at the same time our hearts affirm that there is something authentic about them. In John's gospel Jesus is seen as one who knows more than anyone else about food that satisfies the inner core of our being. Once, when his disciples prevail on him to eat because they're aware that he hasn't done so for a long time, he answers: "I have food to eat that you do not know about. . . . My food is to do the will of him who sent me and to complete his work" (John 4:31–34). Purpose and meaning and mission—all of these feed the soul.

Why have I used the word "banquet" in the title of this book? For me, it conjures up images of abundance, celebrative joy, and generous sharing. Just such experiences are conveyed by Luke's description of meals held in the early Jerusalem church. One biblical scholar, John Navone, has suggested that as the inhabitants of Jerusalem were trying to categorize this new group of Jesus' devotees in their midst, they might well have come up with a term like "banquet community."[15] Their use of that term wouldn't necessarily imply that huge amounts of food and drink were being served in the homes of believers. In fact, that probably wasn't the case since most disciples were people of modest means who couldn't afford lavish menus every day. Instead, the word "banquet" would have denoted both the great frequency of meal

Mutual Honor Abounding

rituals in this community and their joyful character. Eating together with praise and thanksgiving was a special mark of the first church's identity, and it was visible to all (Acts 2:46–47).

Webster's Collegiate Dictionary defines a banquet as "an elaborate and often ceremonious meal for numerous people, often honoring a person." This picture is consistent with what we know about the symposium meals of the first century Greco-Roman world.[16] But at certain points meal settings described in the New Testament seem to push the envelope beyond conventional hellenistic practices. For example, symposia typically welcomed as guests only those invited beforehand. By contrast, when Jesus wants to describe God's kingdom, he tells a parable in which the royal host at a wedding feast, after suffering rebuffs from his invited guests, orders his servants to go into the streets and bring back everyone they find. The result, in Matthew's version of the parable, is that the servants "gathered all whom they found, both good and bad; so the wedding hall was filled with guests" (Matt 22:8–10; see also Luke 14:13). In other words, the banquet of God's kingdom, by its very nature, breaks with convention. Invited guests are welcomed, but so are the uninvited. By reaching out to draw all sorts and conditions into the celebration, God's banquet challenges our church-related meals to "do likewise."

Paul's writings show us another way in which ordinary banquet practices get stretched. We have all sat through ceremonial meals where individuals or groups were honored—sometimes at great length. Such rituals were also well known in the symposia of the ancient world. But Paul insists that at the Lord's Supper honor flows constantly to and from all parties. God is honored through the praise and thanksgiving of the community. At the same time God and Christ are distributing gifts to everyone present through the Holy Spirit, with the result that all worshipers are inspired to honor their neighbors with mutual service (1 Cor 11–14; Rom 12).[17] The evangelist John's version of this reciprocal honoring occurs in his story of the footwashing at Jesus' Last Supper with his disciples (John 13:1–17). Here Jesus the teacher kneels to serve his disciples and then counsels them to love one another in this same manner. In the ancient world honor was usually thought to be a scarce commodity. But when Jesus and the Spirit take charge at the table, honor abounds for all participants.

In his narration of Jesus' Last Supper, Luke provides us with still another image of outreach through a banquet that is best termed counter-cultural. Even as the Lord faces his death, he promises those who are dining with him that at some future date he will grant them a kingdom or ruling office so that they may "eat and drink at my table in my kingdom, and . . . sit on thrones judging the twelve tribes of Israel" (Luke 22:30). Given Luke's understanding of the last things, this ruling activity probably designates not the final judgment at the very end of time but the church's role, beginning at Pentecost, as the vanguard in Israel's restoration.[18] Judging refers to the leadership role that Jesus' disciples will exercise in the tradition of Israel's ancient judges, like Deborah and Gideon. After their empowerment by the Spirit at Pentecost, the disciples lead by preaching, teaching, and healing, mostly apart from and in opposition to the recognized leadership of the temple authorities (Acts 3–6). The rule of Jesus himself, symbolized by his table, discloses itself in a wide range of missionary events involving meals, many of them narrated in the book of Acts. In all of these stories the implicit claim is that what believers do at the table of Jesus contributes mightily to the world's redemption.[19] While the prophet Isaiah and some rabbinic teachers envision a great feast that God will offer to all peoples at the end of days (see Isa 25:6–10), the New Testament writers see this already beginning to happen as a missionary process in the table ministries of Jesus and the church.

These are very big claims. In fact, some may wonder if they are actually true in any practical sense of the word. And even if they are, we may doubt our ability to connect them with the real-life meal practices of our congregations. Here a little skepticism and a lot of humility seem called for. And yet, the deeper meanings of the communal eating and drinking we've just examined lie so close to the heart of the New Testament message—not to mention the church's missionary experience in subsequent centuries—that we're likely to cheat ourselves if we fail to look for them in our own meal settings.

A Meal to Remember

We can begin this discernment process right after we've made our rudimentary list of the meal events now taking place in our congregation.

BIHN night 2X

vegetarian

BIHN

— the way in which banquets break down —

of at church

A good way to start is by asking ourselves if one event on the list stands out in our collective memory as being unusually graced, or even unique. My experience has been that, far from being stunned by this exercise, we'll often come up with two or three candidates. If that happens, we'll find ourselves well on the way toward fine-tuning our capacities for discernment, and the connections we've already looked at in this chapter between scripture and tradition on the one hand and our congregational meals on the other probably won't be so difficult to make after all. Consider this example.

At St. James Church on Madison Avenue, a large congregation in Manhattan with many resources and a strong commitment to missionary outreach, one festival meal from the recent past continues to occupy a special place in the hearts of parishioners. The meal, which took place in October of 2002, seemed both familiar and strange at the same time. Some members who attended thought of it simply as the annual fall stewardship dinner, a St. James tradition for many years. But this dinner differed radically from all its predecessors, because it was held in the huge nave of the newly reconstructed church rather than the undercroft or basement, its usual location.

A combination of circumstances led the church's rector, Brenda Husson, and her vestry to choose the sanctuary for this major programmatic meal. For one thing, the construction project wasn't altogether completed, which meant that no working kitchen existed in the undercroft. More important, however, was the longing of the people to reclaim their main worship space after being absent from it for more than a year. The nave itself wasn't finished yet—the flooring hadn't gone in and there were no pews. But it could be cleaned up sufficiently for the installation of temporary tables and chairs. One parishioner told me: "We needed this homecoming in the worst way. Our dear old church home wasn't there to comfort us when the Trade Center buildings went down on 9/11, because reconstruction had already begun by then. We needed to welcome our sanctuary back and be welcomed by it, even if it was less than perfect." Apparently many people felt this way, since more than three hundred showed up for the meal—a record attendance.

The physical surroundings that night became etched in the memories of many parishioners, along with certain details about what happened at their individual tables. Outside on the streets of Manhattan it was cool and rainy; with no heat in the sanctuary some people wore coats or sweaters as they sat down to eat. Water dribbled through a few small holes in the roof that hadn't yet been sealed. Construction dust, with its distinctive odor, still covered parts of the concrete floor. This was definitely not the heavenly banquet, where all things have been brought to perfection! On the other hand, members found gleaming white cloths on their tables, each adorned with a festive cornucopia and several small votive candles. Pledge cards were located at every place setting.

The food and drink were professionally catered, but a large group of members helped with the serving and clean-up operations, lending a homey touch to the event. Some attendees reported that at the beginning they felt a little uneasy about eating in the sanctuary, not to mention drinking a glass of wine and talking in ordinary tones with their friends. But the atmosphere of joyful reunion quickly overcame their discomfort. The evening's speaker, a well-known Presbyterian minister, talked about gratitude and commitment, not at the end of the meal but during the course of it. When I asked parishioners about what he said, they mostly recalled his tone, which was informal but inspirational and filled with personal testimonies.

Nearly everyone I spoke with seemed deeply affected that evening by an extraordinary visual experience. Some even interpreted it as a kind of revelation. While the nave remained in semi-darkness throughout the dinner, with only the small candles at each table providing light, the altar end of the church was ablaze with glory. Large spotlights had been trained on the chancel, and the result was that the ornate golden *reredos*, the massive carved wood screen directly behind the altar, stood out more boldly than anyone could remember. People describing it to me used words like "mysterious," "regal," and "surreal." Although no one said so directly, my guess is that these adjectives referred chiefly to the larger than life-sized figure of the risen Jesus at the very center of the *reredos*. Surrounded by saints and angels, he stands there majestically, clothed in white and extending both arms in blessing. Whether church leaders intended it or not, illuminating this figure sent a powerful message to the diners.

But what was it exactly? As far as I have been able to tell, no supernatural voice issued directly from the reredos, nor from any other part of the church. And yet at least five New Testament writers insist that the Risen One is regularly present in and with his followers when they gather around tables for meals (see Matt 18:20; Luke 22:14–19; John 17:20–26; 1 Cor 11:17–34; Rev 3:20–22). If we accept this scriptural witness as a true picture of what also happens in our communities today, we can guess that some members of St. James did hear words of Christ in their hearts, words on the order of: "Here you are, my beloved people, back in your church building again, thankfully planning your congregation's new ventures. As you celebrate this homecoming, please know that you are eating and drinking in my presence, at my table, receiving the Spirit that I pour out upon you."

Is this an over-interpretation? Perhaps. But the actual reflections of those attending this dinner seem consistent with it. One person told me: "I felt immense gratitude, not only for being back in our own space again but even more for the discovery that most of my brothers and sisters of the parish hadn't been lost in transition." Another said: "More than any other event, this dinner in the church itself helped me see that what we do in daily life is sacred." A third person told me: "We were definitely being caught up in something bigger than ourselves." Still another reported that for him, the dinner marked a new beginning of abundance and sharing at St. James. "We were being *enticed* into mission," he said, choosing his words carefully.

Here, I think, was a true soul banquet, with its mission-meal synergy fully operative. We might also call it a "graced" event because of the greater than human power for good that seemed to infuse it. In fact, there is much more to say about how this biblical adjective applies to gatherings for food and drink, not only in the New Testament writings but also in the real lives of our congregations. To the fuller meanings of mealtime grace we now turn.

CHAPTER TWO

Gifts at the Table

We Christians have found a host of ways to express the sense of giftedness that permeates our faith. In fact, we usually say that faith itself—entrusting ourselves to God's love through Jesus—is pure gift, not something we can conjure up in ourselves. It comes to us, even as we reach out to claim it for our own, by the unmerited favor or grace of God—*charis* in the Greek New Testament writings. Curiously, this grace of God can also *return* to God through expressions of human thankfulness. On occasion the very same word, *charis*, denotes both gift and response. In 2 Corinthians 9:14–15, for example, Paul tells his readers that the church in Jerusalem is praying for them "because of the surpassing grace of God (*charis*) that he has given you," a thought that then prompts him to exclaim: "Thanks be to God (*charis to theo*) for his indescribable gift!"

Usually, however, the New Testament writers use some form of the Greek word *eucharistia* to describe human acts or words or feelings of thanksgiving. This term appears to be constructed from *charis* and the prefix *eu*, meaning good or well; so the literal translation would be something like "a speaking well of grace." The verb for "giving thanks," *eucharistein*, occurs in all four of the New Testament stories describing Jesus' ritual actions at the Last Supper. It also appears in Paul's comments on community meals in Rome (14:6); in John's version of the feeding of the five thousand (6:11, 23); and in Luke's story of Paul, the seafaring prisoner, who thanks God publicly as he breaks bread in the midst of a life-threatening storm, thereby encouraging his frightened and seasick shipmates to eat as well (Acts 27:35f.). Early on in the New

Testament period, thanking God came to be seen as a central act in the meals of the church, even when they were not ritual commemorations of the Last Supper as such (Acts 2:46f.). This phenomenon suggests that New Testament believers felt unusually gifted by God when they shared food together—a matter to which we shall return.

Grace and Charisma

About the middle of the first century CE a new word for gift, *charisma*, begins to surface with some regularity in the Greek language.[1] It's formed from *charis* and the little suffix *ma* and denotes a particular manifestation of grace or favor. We find this term at least once in Philo, the great Jewish philosopher of Alexandria (ca. 35 BCE– 45 CE). But it is most widely attested in Paul's letters, and it may well be the apostle who first gave it the connotation best known to us today—a special divine gift that confers power on the person receiving it.

For Paul, the word usually points to a particular "package" of grace or a grace-infused event. Historical particularity rather than God's universal good will is emphasized. For example, Paul thinks of the ability to marry, or to remain chastely unmarried, as a *charisma* (1 Cor 7:7). Today we tend to label such matters "lifestyle choices" that result from various combinations of heredity and environment. But in Paul's view it is God who bestows special talents for the married or unmarried state. Choice remains, but it is experienced as an act surrounded by blessing. When the apostle gives his readers advice on gatherings for worship, he frequently uses the word *charisma* to name special energies of the Holy Spirit that manifest themselves in individuals. These include speaking in tongues, prophecy, and healing but also less spectacular activities like teaching and the regular showing of compassion (1 Cor 12:4, 9, 28, 30–31; Rom 12:3–8.). Here again the key words are ability and blessing, for the people who receive such gifts retain a large degree of freedom regarding their use or non-use (1 Cor 26–33).

For Paul and Philo alike, *charisma* was not to be understood as an innate human quality, a magnetic force of the personality, perhaps, that enables an individual to exercise dominance in a group. Only from the early twentieth century onward, under the influence of the sociologist Max Weber, have we come to think of *charisma* as a rare trait, limited to successful leaders.[2] Today we often use the word to describe politicians and other high-profile people, like actors and athletes, who stand out from the masses. I have even seen the term applied to a line of towels and a brand of costume jewelry.

To their credit, Roman Catholic authors have usually preserved a more biblical understanding of the term, often using its Latin form, "charism," to denote special gifts for ministry that manifest themselves in religious communities or individuals. On this view, grace-gifts are broadly distributed, appearing often in leaders and followers alike. That comes close to Paul's use of *charisma* in his letters; but the apostle is even more democratic. For him, all believers, and all Jews, regardless of whether they believe in Jesus as Messiah (Rom 11:29), may exercise charismatic power. This takes many forms but always serves to express God's transforming love for humanity through human words and actions. *Charisma* is about mutual service, about developing relationships through which we honor and strengthen one another. Early in his epistle to the Romans Paul writes: "I am longing to see you so that I may share some spiritual gift (*charisma*) to strengthen you—or rather so that we may be mutually encouraged by each other's faith, both yours and mine" (1:11–12). Here the Greek term may refer to faith stories as well as actions.

Paul's fullest discourse on *charismata* (the plural of *charisma*) occurs in his first letter to the Corinthians, where the chief problem addressed has to do with what the apostle takes to be the prideful disregard and even contempt that many Corinthians show toward some of their sister and brother believers, whom they regard as less gifted than themselves. How contemporary this sounds! Paul's repeated admonition to the proud Corinthians, expressed in different ways throughout chapters 12–14 of his epistle, is that God bestows grace-gifts on all believers. Though some may appear inferior to others, that is not so in the eyes of God, who characteristically exalts people whom the world dismisses as useless or insignificant. Paul would have applauded the words of Mary's Magnificat: "He has shown strength with his arm; he has scattered the proud in the thoughts of their hearts. He has brought down the powerful from their thrones, and lifted up the lowly" (Luke 1:51–52. For Paul's own version of this grand confession, see 1 Corinthians 1:26f.).

God desires that in communities of believers each person's gifts will be recognized with gratitude and used lovingly to build up the whole body of Christ for its mission (see especially 1 Corinthians 13, Paul's great chapter on *agape* love). Here are some of the apostle's choice words on the subject:

> Now there are varieties of gifts (*charismata*), but the same Spirit; and there are varieties of services, but the same Lord; and there are varieties of activities, but it is the same God who activates them all in everyone. To each is given the manifestation of the Spirit for the common good (12:4–7). . . . if I have prophetic powers, and understand all mysteries and all knowledge, and if I have all faith, so as to remove mountains, but do not have love (*agape*), I am nothing (13:2). . . . When you come together, each one has a hymn, a lesson, a revelation, a tongue, or an interpretation. Let all things be done for building up (14:26f.).

If we read through the entire three-chapter discourse in which these passages occur, it becomes clear that the gifts Paul focuses on (because he thinks they are being abused) have to do mostly with how believers express themselves in corporate worship.

Can we be more specific about how the *charismata* named in 1 Corinthians 12–14 were functioning within first-century communities of believers? We can, but Christians in the mainline and liberal churches might find this focus troubling, because to a large degree it supports versions of faith and worship favored by Pentecostal believers. For example, Paul insists that the Holy Spirit, who is closely linked with the risen Jesus, actively and regularly bestows gifts on all participants in the worship assembly (1 Cor 12:11). Many of these gifts are verbal expressions of messages from God delivered though particular individuals (prophecy, glossolalia, utterances of wisdom, utterances of knowledge, teachings, prayers in the Spirit).[3]

We need not assume, as many Pentecostal believers do, that all of these were oracular in style—introduced by some form of the sentence: "Thus says the Lord." Nor did the verbal gifts need to be transmitted in a loud voice. In our day we can point to the Quakers, who are known for speaking God's word with quiet authority and often after long periods of silence. We should also consider the fact that first-century believers didn't necessarily accept all words spoken or sung "in the Spirit" as authentic communications direct from heaven. Paul, for example, outlines a process of discernment in which no individual prophecy is assumed to contain the whole truth on a given matter (see 1 Corinthians 13:9; 14:29f.).

Certain *charismata* and *pneumatika*—an equivalent term meaning literally "things of the Spirit" (1 Cor 12:1; 14:1; Rom 15:27)—have to do with deeds of power. Among them are events of physical healing (see 1 Corinthians 12:9–10). But here again we shouldn't get hung up on the notion that all these activities looked spectacular or miraculous, or that they always commanded everyone's immediate attention or happened instantaneously. In 2 Corinthians 1:8–11 Paul refers to a time when he gained release from prison as a *charisma* from God. For the apostle, this new freedom was truly a grace-gift, even though it manifested itself gradually through the bureaucratic process of Roman law.[4]

The qualifying statements I've just presented may help us mainline Christians relax a little when it comes to New Testament descriptions of charismatic gifts in action. But I doubt whether they can entirely eliminate the discomfort we're likely to feel every time we try to imagine what Sunday services in our home church might look like if they included the exchanges of words and touches among participants envisioned by Paul. As an Episcopalian who remains captivated by the dignified language in our Book of Common Prayer, I share these apprehensions. Still, we need to open ourselves to the flow of the Spirit's guidance if we expect the faith and missionary outreach of our churches to grow stronger.

In his letter to believers in Rome the apostle presents a slightly different, though no less challenging, perspective on the emergence and practice of *charismata* in the community's worship. He begins what we now call the twelfth chapter of Romans with an appeal to his readers to offer their bodies "as a living sacrifice, holy and acceptable to God, which is your spiritual worship" (12:1). He continues by urging his addressees to "be transformed by the renewing of your minds" (12:2) and then explains that a major feature of this ongoing change consists of not thinking "more highly [about yourself] than you ought to think" but rather considering the self "with sober judgment, each according to the measure of faith that God has assigned" (12:3). Paul next repeats something he had earlier told the Corinthians—that we are all one body in Christ (12:5)—and adds, again paralleling 1 Corinthians, that we all receive gifts to offer one another in our congregational assemblies:

> We have gifts (*charismata*) that differ according to the grace (*charis*) given to us: prophecy, in proportion to faith; ministry, in ministering; the teacher, in teaching; the exhorter, in exhortation; the giver [literally, "distributor"], in generosity; the leader [or patron] in diligence; the compassionate, in cheerfulness (12:6–8).

Without trying to define exactly which virtues and talents are being highlighted here,[5] we notice right away that, except for prophecy, these charismata look rather less spectacular than those enumerated in 1 Corinthians. They are aptitudes for the long haul, for daily life.

I think Paul is always trying to impress his readers with the endless variety of charismatic gifts. He wants them to know they can never write out an exhaustive list of gifts (see Romans 11:33–36). Brand-new ones will always appear as surprises. Thus, charismatic gifts can seem extraordinary by society's standards, or they can look quite ordinary, almost insignificant. But whatever form they take, the eyes of faith will see the grace of God at work in them, and expressions of thanksgiving will eventually follow (1 Cor 14:15–17). Paul believes that all of this discerning and claiming and exercising and thanking typically happens when believers gather for worship to offer themselves to God (Rom 12:1).

Gift Exchange in the Dining Room

But here again we need to get more specific. Just what kind of worship are we talking about? Above all, I think, it's worship that takes place during meals. When Paul spells out his views on problems connected with the practice of the Lord's Supper in Corinth (1 Cor 11:17–34), he presupposes that the emergence and use of spiritual gifts, which he goes on to discuss at length in chapters 12–14, will be a regular part of his readers' experience *at the table.* But this wasn't just a Corinthian phenomenon. In fact, we should probably consider the weekly ritual meals of most New Testament churches to be the normal settings for receiving divine *charismata.*[6] As Paul envisioned the worship event in Corinth, people normally gathered for an evening meal at which bread and wine were served. During this "Lord's Supper," participants allowed for special moments in which they recalled and prayed about Christ's death, resurrection, and coming again. They did so with much gratitude because these realities were transforming their lives. Some of the prayers at table commemorated (but probably didn't try to replicate) Jesus' Last Supper with his disciples.[7] We don't know much about the content of these earliest "eucharistic" prayers, but Paul does tell us that special blessings were said over the bread and wine (1 Cor 10:16). Almost certainly they included references to Jesus' saving work. Throughout the meal, Paul thinks, the presence of Jesus as Regent of God's kingdom loomed large, even when worshipers were not aware of it (1 Cor 11:27–32 understood in the light of 15:20–28).

At certain times during the supper, perhaps between courses or toward the end, or both, participants became especially receptive to the manifestation of charismatic gifts.[8] Paul simply assumes that this is the normal practice in Corinth and endorses it, but he also gives advice for ordering the worship so that all participants will be honored and built up, not just a few (1 Cor 14). The gifts mentioned include inspired blessings, thanksgivings, prophecies, hymns, and teachings, some of which could well have blended with prayers of commemoration. Other gifts, like healing, probably involved both prayer and the laying on of hands (Jas 5:14). Greeting one another with a "holy kiss" (1 Cor 16:20) obviously involved some kind of touching, perhaps an embrace. The practice could well have symbolized gratitude for the gifts of God perceived in others, as well as a gesture of affection. Acts of reconciliation in the worship assembly between people who had suffered through times of estrangement from one another (Jas 5:16) would almost certainly involve physical contact. All of this suggests that we ought to imagine people moving around the dining room with some frequency instead of being fixed in their places during the ritual.

In Corinth, and probably most other New Testament churches as well, the meal that Paul calls "Lord's Supper" was a very fluid affair, with considerable activity on the part of the participants and a variety of charismatic phenomena in evidence. In fact, one of the apostle's big concerns as he writes to the Corinthians is that their worship dare not look like total confusion to those who come as visitors, since they are potential converts (1 Cor 14:23–25). Thus Paul advises his readers that all things "should be done decently and in order" (1 Cor 14:40). But even as he does so, he clearly wishes to affirm the spontaneity of the Spirit he has been describing throughout chapters 12–14. My guess is that Paul would find the ordering of Sunday services in our mainline churches much too rigid.

What can we say about the worship in Rome that Paul links with the practice of charismatic gifts? In *The Feast of the World's Redemption* I have tried to show that in composing the twelfth chapter of his epistle to the Romans the apostle imagines a Lord's Supper-type meal for the enacting of his counsel, just as he does in 1 Corinthians 12–14.[9] We shouldn't suppose that he thinks of prophecy, teaching, exhorting, and so on as activities *confined* to times of ritual eating and drinking. That would mean straight-jacketing the Spirit. But for Paul and many other New Testament believers, I'm now convinced, the mysteries of God's *charismata* were most regularly experienced during worship at table.[10] The gifts manifested themselves first for community upbuilding, but by their very nature they also spilled out into daily encounters with non-believers and became missionary in character (see Acts 4:23–31).

Discerning Our Gifts

One hugely important gift that the apostle wants all his readers to claim and use throughout the course of their meal gatherings, especially during the blessings over bread and wine, is what he calls "discerning the body" (1 Cor 11:29). This doesn't mean, primarily, making an act of devotion to honor the consecrated bread. Nor does it mean trying very hard to believe in Christ's sacramental presence so that we'll be worthy enough to eat and drink at the holy meal. Instead, as most commentators now agree, Paul's reference to "the body" in this context has to do especially with the body of Christ composed of everyone participating in the meal (12:12–13, 27). These people, as believers, have come together to eat and drink with Jesus and also to commune with one another. This they do (or should do), Paul thinks, through giving and receiving spiritual gifts. In his view, the Holy Spirit constantly channels abundant resources to some believers so that they can minister to the limitations and needs borne by others, with the result that all parties are built up and honored. Moreover, in God's wisdom, the "some" and the "others" are frequently trading places within the church so that those occupying official positions of leadership aren't necessarily the centers of power (see 1 Corinthians 12:4–26 and 14:3–26).

To live comfortably within this dynamic form of gift exchange is a tall order. Real communities of believers, whether in first-century Corinth and Rome, or in the twenty-first century, have always found it difficult to approach the biblical ideal. When that does happen, God's grace turns out to be the primary cause. I remember a moment, some years ago during a Eucharist, when I was struggling with personal issues of pride and humiliation—a familiar duo in my experience. As I walked back to my seat in the nave after receiving the bread and wine, my eyes were opened to everyone present in a way that seemed to me altogether new. This is how I put it at the time:

> I see now that I cannot be separate in the Lord from these, my brothers and sisters. They are sharers in Christ's body, as real and valuable as I am. I am neither more nor less than they, but only different. I cannot use what the world counts as advantage against these people. We exist as partners, and we need one another for the sake of our very lives.[11]

This little "vision" actually helped me to seek mutuality with members of my church at a deeper level than I had ever done before. It helped me truly to value these others and give thanks for them—even the ones I didn't like very well. Although I didn't know precisely *how* each of them was gifted for the sake of us all, I was coming to see that their gifts were real and that a part of my vocation was to search them out, extending honor to their bearers in brand new ways. I think a lot about this moment of discernment, this gift in the twinkling of an eye. I now try to make it a regular practice, not only at Eucharists but at other meals as well.

Sometimes, though, I'm hindered in my eucharistic worship because I can't easily see the faces of my sisters and brothers. Rigid seating and kneeling arrangements create obstacles. In addition, I find it hard to remember and claim insights that bubble up in my consciousness during the Holy Communion because there's no place in the liturgy itself for sharing them. Occasionally I've found coffee hours to be the right occasions for making contact with my gifted co-worshipers, for talking about what we might do together as charismatic people. But it doesn't seem to be enough. Now that I'm convinced by my own research on the spontaneity of eucharistic worship in the New Testament churches, I'm constantly on the lookout for missionary callings and empowerings right in the midst of the liturgy. And they do come, but I mostly just let them go. I suspect that some readers know what it means to feel their own eucharistic visions and insights melting away all too quickly, before they can be acted upon. Even worse, some will quickly conclude, as I've often done, that these revelations weren't very important anyway. How easily we diminish ourselves, precisely in the receiving of grace gifts; and then we project that self-assessment onto others. Yet the Risen One keeps after us because he wants our stature as missionary disciples to become more solid, not less, as we enter into his own real presence at the table.

Meals and Mission at the Church of the Saviour

It could be that for many church members these days a serious exploration of missionary gifts in meal settings will have to begin with those occurring outside our formal liturgies. The lay theologian Elizabeth O'Connor has given us some good counsel on these matters, based on her experience at the Church of the Saviour in Washington, D.C. In her books *Eighth Day of Creation* and *The New Community* she offers some arresting stories about what happened when "mission groups" of the congregation served out their rotation as hosts at the Potter's House, a coffee shop on Columbus Road established soon after the community's founding in 1946 to initiate contact with its neighbors.

Extremely important, I think, is O'Connor's observation that mission groups typically come into being only when particular church members hear a call to ministry and are able to express it in such a way that it sounds like good news to others. All those inspired by this message then respond by joining the initiators, working together with them on specific goals. O'Connor notes that "when a new group comes into existence, one of its first tasks is to identify the gifts of each of its members so that every person is exercising a gift on behalf of the group."[12] For believers at the Church of the Saviour, "call" and "gift" are closely linked. People feel the need to speak of them as a unity, as a kind of gospel-centered appeal to action.

Such appeals sound very much like what Paul calls prophecy, especially those forms of it occurring at the Lord's Supper in Corinth. For him, the chief fruit of this most important charisma is *paraklesis* (see 1 Corinthians 14:3, 31), which we can translate as both "exhortation" (Do this . . .) and "encouragement" (You have the power to do this . . .). New Testament prophecy plays a major role in the church's missionary activity because the prophet speaks to people's hearts about God's gifts and callings (1 Cor 14:25). I've come to think that an openness to prophecy on our part, especially when it occurs at table, can contribute immensely to the renewal of our congregational life. So frequently we suffer from paralysis (the opposite of *paraklesis*) because we pay more attention to the overwhelming needs of the world than to the Spirit's guidance and potency in our midst. How will we hear the voice of the Spirit? It won't necessarily be noisy or long-winded. It may well occur within sermons or in a short sentence spoken almost matter-of-factly by one of our companions during a congregational meal.

O'Connor narrates a shift in the Church of the Saviour's outreach ministry that illustrates the Pauline model of prophecy through table talk. Some years ago, when some of those who regularly staffed the Potter's House became more aware of the depressing ghetto in the back streets surrounding their coffee shop, they

turned their thoughts to the massive problem of housing in the District. It seemed to them that the best way to eradicate the creeping blight and decay of the city was to purchase housing in the area, to work with the tenants to upgrade it without raising rents, and then to begin a program of education, literacy, recreation, and counseling that would engender hope and spread to the larger community. The more they talked the larger grew the vision. . . . Though the members of the Thursday night group half guessed that this would mean some sharing of the wealth. . . , they had very little idea then . . . of how this might affect any of our community, or whether we were ready for it in any significant way. The new mission, nonetheless took the name of Jubilee Housing. . . .[13]

Next to these words in O'Connor's book, *The New Community*, is a photo. It shows members of the Thursday mission group sitting around a dinner table in the Potter's House and bears the caption: "The more they talked the larger grew the vision." What the photo itself doesn't reveal (but O'Connor later tells us) is that while some of those gathered at the table were hosts—church members and friends staffing the Potter's House—others were guests, people from the neighborhood who felt drawn into the mealtime planning as they drank their coffee at nearby tables and overheard some of their deepest needs and hopes being addressed.

The Thursday group eventually persuaded others in the church that God was calling Jubilee Housing to purchase two run-down apartment buildings named the Ritz and the Mozart, which were located a few streets away from the Potter's House. But since the church had little money, not much happened until

One night [the Thursday group] shared their wild ideas with a friend who dropped by for coffee. He, a mortgage banker who had worked all his life with real estate, had some wild dreams of his own for the renewal of cities. . . . It was easy for him to fall in with the spirit of the group and to offer to arrange the loan for the down payment. . . .[14]

A lucky break? Or the guidance of the Spirit? Church members tended toward the latter interpretation. To make a long story short, Jubilee Housing eventually managed not only to purchase the apartment buildings but also, through persistent efforts that stretched over two years and involved cooperation with most of the existing tenants, to renovate them.

During this period the young organization, which kept expanding to include more people from the neighborhood, plus groups from other churches close by, began to gather every other week at the Potter's House for an evening meal followed by prayer and celebration. Participants called these meals Ram's Horn Feasts, deriving the name from Old Testament accounts of the trumpet that was blown to inaugurate Israel's Jubilee Year (Lev 25:8–11) and also from the well-known battle of Jericho story in which blasts from Israel's shofars are said to have caused the city's walls to fall (Josh 6:1–20).

Elizabeth O'Connor reports that the dinners were usually prepared and served by children living in the renovated apartments who had learned cooking skills from mission group members and organized themselves into the Ritzart Bakery and Catering Services. O'Connor describes the common meals this way:

> The community that gathers for the Ram's Horn Feast is made up of a great diversity of persons. . . . A few like to speak in intellectual terms, and a few like to speak in tongues. We are from churches housed in storefronts and from churches with impressive towers . . . we meet to celebrate our common humanity and to read and ponder Scripture and to wait for the empowering of the Spirit. . . . We do a lot of talking about houses, and community building, and a world that is divinely marked for salvation.[15]

While these dinner gatherings were not explicitly called Eucharists or Lord's Suppers, it seems clear that many of the things New Testament believers expected to happen during their ritual meals did in fact take place here in the Potter's House. Above all, in an atmosphere where people longed for redemptive change, the Spirit of Christ granted gifts and callings that evolved into mission.

Some readers may be wondering whether the various meals and kaffee klatsches associated with the Potter's House are really essential to the Church of the Saviour's missionary activity, or just a nice extra touch that facilitates it. And of course some readers may also be wondering if this same question applies to their own home congregations.

Clearly, I come down on the "essentialist" side of things—not because I can prove that position beyond a shadow of a doubt but because the weight of the New Testament evidence regarding meals in Jesus' ministry and the outreach activities of the earliest churches is so strong. Indeed, we can add to that evidence the experience of many contemporary churches that are undergoing renewal.[16]

Discernment at Table in Four Mainline Churches

One such community is the Zionsville Presbyterian Church, near Indianapolis. The pastor of this rapidly growing congregation, Glenn McDonald, has joined with Columbia Seminary professor Ben Campbell Johnson to write a guidebook for U.S. Christians based on the corporate faith journey of believers in his church and in a few others. The two authors call their volume *Imagining a Church in the Spirit: A Task for Mainline Congregations*. Like believers associated with the Church of the Saviour, members of Zionsville Presbyterian put great stock in the importance of spiritual gifts for initiating and empowering outreach ministries. The congregation sponsors a number of small groups for helping people to identify and claim their gifts, especially if they are newcomers. The authors write, perceptively, that:

> Discerning gifts is far more than checking a list of time and talents. Discernment of gifts has a clear focus on the God who created these particular persons and gave them gifts. Also, discernment is about the Holy Spirit, who gives special capabilities to the people of God. Discernment seldom comes instantaneously but requires life to be lived in a community over a period of time.[17]

McDonald and Johnson don't single out the Lord's Supper or other meals as special opportunities for discerning gifts, but they define the Eucharist as an "actual communion with the living Lord" and "the continual reception of [Christ's] life-giving presence."[18] When we put these confessional statements together with their observation later in the book that "discernment of call will force the church to deal directly with the risen Lord,"[19] I think we can infer that, for McDonald and

recognizing the the Holy k in people and for the
signs of the Spirit at work plan of God
yes, in worship

Gifts at the Table   33

Johnson, celebrations of the Lord's Supper will become occasions for hearing and responding to calls from Christ.

But such calls come also in church-related meals apart from the Lord's Supper. A story told by Ben Johnson highlights the importance of small group dinners in a communal discernment process that took place at Glendale Presbyterian Church in California. Jan, a young mother who had recently joined the church, soon recognized that she was not the only newcomer who needed to make more meaningful connections with long-term members. Through one of her pastor's sermons, which stressed that God often speaks to us by repeated messages from varied sources, Jan heard a personal call to help create the needed connections. She decided to test out an idea she had been mulling over for a special Bible study group composed of both new and older members. This, she imagined, might be just the thing to promote significant relationships between the two groups.

Jan talked first to a good friend, who affirmed her idea with enthusiasm, and then to three couples with whom she met monthly for food and fellowship. Only when she had received *their* support, which came with caveats that were explored over dinner, did she feel encouraged enough to approach the pastor and governing body of the church for a discussion. Soon after this meeting, a group much like the one Jan had envisioned came into being, and the results she hoped for were largely achieved. Here it seems that the "testing at table" (my words) proved decisive in helping Jan mold her idea into a proposal that could be heard as good news by the church's leaders.[20]

At my home parish, St. George's in Rumson, New Jersey, the Rev. Ophelia Laughlin chose to reflect on the beginning of her sixth year as rector by sending an e-mail on the topic of discernment to every member of the congregation. I thought the title that she created for her message, from Ezekiel 36:26, was strikingly apt: "A new heart I will give you and a new spirit I will put within you." In her e-mail Ophelia wrote that as she was thinking about how all of us might go forward into the future together at St. George's, it came to her that an increased emphasis on spirituality was needed. "I am convinced," she wrote, "that prayer holds the answer, and to that end, I am inviting all those interested to share an hour's time of prayer and breakfast with me on Saturday . . . at 8:30 a.m. [three weeks hence]." St. George's is a busy suburban parish, full of commuters and young families with active children, so it was a risky move to ask people who prize their weekends to give up an early Saturday morning. But they came in large numbers. In fact, a good cross-section of the congregation showed up, many of them bringing hot dishes for the meal in the parish hall.

Breakfast itself was first on the agenda, and along with it came a bonding among members that didn't typically happen in other situations. Ophelia thinks that the setting was special for people, because they felt they were committing themselves to the real work of the church. As breakfast ended, the rector posed three questions for parishioners to reflect on in silence, both in relation to their personal lives and to the life of the congregation: 1) Where has Jesus been for you in the past five years at St. George's? 2) How is Jesus present with you now? 3) Where do you think Jesus is leading you and our church? After a short pause, the group was asked to pray out loud together a petition for discernment attributed to Vasily Drosdov Philaret, a nineteenth-century Russian Orthodox *staretz*, or holy man. The first and last verses of the prayer go like this:

O Lord, we do not know what to ask you.
You alone know our real needs, and you love us more
than we even know how to love.
Enable us to discern our true needs, which are hidden from us. . . .
We offer ourselves in sacrifice to you and put all our trust in you.
We desire only to do your will.
Teach us how to pray and pray in us, yourself.

As is common in Orthodox circles, this prayer addresses the Holy Trinity. Some readers will recognize that the final sentence derives both from Luke 11:1, where the disciples say to Jesus: "Lord, teach us to pray," and from Romans 8:26–27, where Paul names the Holy Spirit dwelling within us as the One who helps us and intercedes for us when we don't know how to pray.

After the breakfast group had offered this petition for discernment, more silence followed, and then a conversation began. The first comments were questions about how one could know when a prayer was being answered and how this particular gathering might come to a consensus about what God wanted for St. George's. Needless to say, total clarity wasn't achieved on these matters. Nevertheless, some parishioners were able to testify to God's guidance in their lives, and a few even ventured to articulate visions for St. George's that sounded much grander than personal wish lists because they incorporated the ministry gifts of other members. Before leaving, everyone present agreed that another meeting of this sort needed to take place again in the near future. As I'm writing these words, a second discernment breakfast is upcoming at St. George's—and this time it's scheduled for one and a half hours.

A fourth instance of discernment at meals in a mainline congregation is really the story of a movement that's happening in many congregations. It's called the Great Banquet (a title based on Jesus' parable in Luke 14:15–24), and its current home base for the Indianapolis area, where I first learned about it, is Second Presbyterian Church. In a brochure promoting this three-day event, local leaders call attention to its evolution from the Roman Catholic Cursillo and the United Methodist Walk to Emmaus program, both of which stress the importance of communal meals for participants. According to the brochure, participants in the Banquet may expect

> a 72-hour experience, beginning on Thursday evening and ending Sunday evening. For three days, guests live and study together in a worshipful time of singing, prayer, and discussion. During each of the 15 talks given by laity and clergy, the theme of God's grace is presented. Guests participate in the daily celebration of Holy Communion and examine more fully the presence of Christ in His body of believers. They personally experience His grace through the prayers and acts of a loving, Christian support community.

Although the word "discernment" doesn't appear as such in this promotional material, the sentence describing Holy Communion as an opportunity for participants to "examine more fully the presence of Christ in His body of believers" is its functional equivalent. The words refer directly to 1 Cor 11:28–29, where Paul urges his readers to "examine" themselves through a process that consists largely of "discerning the body." In other words, those attending the Great Banquet are promised that they'll become aware of Christ's presence in their sisters and brothers in a new way, one that reveals how powerfully gifted they are for ministry.

Consistent with this promise is another section of the brochure, which states that the goal of the Great Banquet is to help participants "live a life of grace and respond to higher levels of Christian discipleship." I haven't been present at a Great Banquet, but when I talked with those who have, they said a lot about experiencing gifts and about thanksgiving as a basis for growth in their Christian lives. Most of them also complimented the director of food services at Second Presbyterian Church for the extraordinary meals she provided. Finally, it's important to note that a co-sponsor of the Great Banquet in Indianapolis is Light of the World Christian Church, a largely African-American congregation with Pentecostal roots. As a consequence, one can hardly imagine that the *charismata* mentioned in 1 Corinthians 12–14 will fail to show up in the communal meals of this three-day event.

A Missionary Lunch in San Jose

Often enough, gifts at the table just appear, with little or no advance planning. Not long ago my wife, Elisabeth, preached at Trinity Episcopal Cathedral in San Jose, California, while I sat in the congregation, worshiping with friends. One of the cathedral canons, John Huntington, had taken it upon himself to host a lunch after church for the visiting preacher and some others. John persists in saying that he had no special agenda for the meal. Still, when I arrived at the restaurant and saw the round table to which we were being led, I had an intimation that something unusual was about to happen. We were a group of eight women and men that included the cathedral's interim Dean and a married couple who had recently renewed their membership in the congregation after a difficult period of leadership changes.

At first, we simply enjoyed one another's company and the food. Then, almost casually, someone mentioned that part of Trinity's "comeback" had to do with a large number of new Hispanic members, who were now moving to establish their own mission parish, though still in collaboration with the cathedral. Someone else followed up by noting a comparable surge in worshipers from another ethnic group, young African men who were mostly refugees from Sudan. What surprised most members of our luncheon group was learning that the majority of these new immigrants were Anglicans, Christians driven from their homes into a nomad existence by feuding factions in the government. As I write, Darfur remains a bitter symbol of this ongoing nightmare. Various international agencies had enabled a number of young people from the Sudan to escape from wretched conditions in refugee camps and find their way to the U.S. But now they needed additional help with food, housing, and jobs, and the cathedral staff was beginning to talk about how they might respond to this new situation.

Just then, one of the two returning members of the congregation spoke up. "I'd like to help," she said. "I have professional skills and resources to contribute. Tell me what to do." In an instant, our luncheon became a planning session. Elisabeth and I remembered that one of our seminary graduates, Mark Nikkel, had devoted his entire adult ministry to Sudanese Christians, personally translating parts of the Bible into the Dinka language before his untimely death in his late thirties. Somehow that memory reinforced the rightness of our developing vision: It was emerging as *our* thing to do, not someone else's. Others at the table quickly thought of more gifts and tasks that would move the ministry forward. Only a few months after the lunch, Elisabeth and I learned from a diocesan newsletter that Trinity's work with Sudanese refugees had, in fact, been launched. It remains a thriving ministry of the cathedral to this day.[21]

What had caused the great leap forward at our table? Was it something communicated through the sermon? Possibly. Elisabeth, a survivor of the 9/11 events at Ground Zero, had spoken eloquently about how fragile our lives are and how precious they are in God's sight. Was the eucharistic meal of the church service somehow continuing into our luncheon? Possibly. The Dean had celebrated beautifully, inviting several laypeople who were being honored for their ministries to join him around the altar for the prayers of consecration. How did everything come together in the way it did? No one knows for sure. But serendipitous things do tend to happen at table in Christian communities—far more than we realize. Perhaps we can dare to claim, in this case, that the Holy Spirit moved us. Ordinary food and drink became a soul banquet, freighted with abundance and a new sense of calling. Gifts emerged, along with commitments to use them. And the mission of the church blossomed.

Chuck –
Asperger's Syndrome

Susan + Stanley
Wood

– Taking time to do
things together
Kitchen clean-up
and fellowship

who is worthy?

CHAPTER THREE

Exploring the Potential of Our Meals

C an we train ourselves to recognize meals in our communities that are already producing gifts for mission, right under our noses? And can we then name these as soul banquets, thanking God for them and celebrating them in the expectation that even more gifts will emerge from them? If we can focus on these goals, we're likely to discover other meals at the edge of our congregation's life that may seem largely secular but are actually charged with possibilities for mission. Conversely, we'll probably find meals close to home that are heavy-laden with Christian symbolism but mostly lacking in missionary force. There's no better way to start our exploration than with a prayerful openness, allowing the Holy Spirit to shape our sensibilities.

With an Eye toward God's Kingdom

As we look for patterns in our congregational meals, we always need at the same time to be seeking the loving reign or kingdom of God, because it's the deep reality that supports both the internal health of our community and its outreach activities. Jesus compared the kingdom to a great banquet, so it comes as a surprise to read in Paul's letter to the Romans that "the kingdom of God is not [about] food and drink but righteousness, peace, and joy in the Holy Spirit" (14:17). This sounds strange because Paul appears to be *detaching* the kingdom and the Spirit from community meals—thus taking a stand against the major thesis of this book—not to mention a clear teaching of Jesus!

Happily most biblical scholars have concluded that we shouldn't take the words of Romans 14:17 in such an oppositional way. James Dunn, for example, writes that while it may seem as though Paul's words about eating and drinking are at odds with Jesus' banquet metaphor, this is really not so. In Dunn's view: "Jesus' parable . . . was a protest against the sort of restrictions on table fellowship which Pharisees and . . . Essenes practiced. Paul is making precisely the same protest against a measuring of what is acceptable in God's presence in terms of rules governing eating and drinking."[1] So we might translate the first part of 14:17 as: "The kingdom of God is not about arguments over what food and drink to serve, when, and to whom."

Looking at the larger context in the Epistle to the Romans helps us gain a clearer understanding of Paul's intent. Verse 17 forms part of a section in which the apostle counsels believers who are in conflict with one another over food purity and calendar issues and can't therefore bring themselves to schedule common meals for the entire community. Paul probably has ritual meals in mind here, because he indicates that they are to take place in the presence of the risen Christ (Rom 14:6). This suggests that the Romans are not celebrating communal Lord's Suppers at which all church members in the city feel welcome. As Paul sees it, any fragmentation of believers into separate table communities that isolate themselves from one another always results in a diminishment of the kingdom's coming for everyone (Rom 14:20). In part, this is because the full range of spiritual gifts that typically manifest themselves at meals will be withheld from the community as a whole. The plenitude of God's "righteousness, joy, and peace in the Holy Spirit" will elude the Romans as long as their small house churches fail to unite for large meal events.

Paul seldom writes about the actual presence of God's reign in human communities here and now, preferring to interpret it as a future time of perfection. Yet here he clearly implies that it breaks into our lives now through the activity of Christ and the Spirit—and precisely when we gather for meals. It's no accident that the great Russian Orthodox theologian Alexander Schmemann chose Romans 14:17 to support his conviction that boundaries between earth and heaven begin to melt away in the celebration of the eucharist.[2] Here is a scriptural call for full participation in table sharing that carries enormous promise.

This promise and the many other biblical references to God's activity at meals encourage us to put a high priority on assessing the potential of our own congregational eating and drinking. A practical way to initiate this process is simply to list all the church-related meals that take place among us with some regularity. Doing so, I think, will probably result in a rather long inventory, surprisingly long for most of our congregations. My friend Robbin Clark, rector of St. Mark's Church in Berkeley, where community meals abound, has given serious thought to how this list-making might go forward most effectively. She suggests that congregations could begin with a workshop or retreat on the subject of meals in the church and that the leaders who need to be brought into the process early on are those charged with ministry development, stewardship, and worship. She also adds, with a twinkle in her eye, that the great cooks and hosts of the congregation should be present.

Another essential feature of our explorations will be the development of criteria for evaluating our meals in terms of their missionary synergy. In the following pages I offer five of these that have evolved from my scriptural studies and from the interviews I've conducted with a number of leaders in North American churches. The criteria are by no means exhaustive but rather indicate the *kind* of things we need to be looking for. They will need to be adapted to the special circumstances of each congregation.

Five Benchmarks for Meals and Mission

1) Meals are served graciously. Criterion number one has to do with the basics, with the food and drink themselves and how they are served. Do we offer wholesome and attractive meals, both to those in great need (perhaps at feeding programs) and to those who are regular members of our congregation? One concern here would be whether the quality of what we serve differs markedly in the two situations. Lyndon Harris of St. Paul's, Ground Zero, was quite intentional about providing the highest quality meals possible to the emergency workers who crowded into his church, and we probably need to ask ourselves whether the "less productive" guests at our feeding programs are necessarily less deserving. A related set of questions focuses on the presentation of meals in the circle of our congregational life, right down to the informal snacks we provide. Can we discern some graciousness in this whole process, some thankful celebration of God's presence? Do we ever put flowers or candles on our tables? Or are things just thrown together, with efficiency as our major objective?

One minister I interviewed suggested that it should be part of the church's countercultural vocation to promote "slow food."³ To her, this means creating opportunities that allow us plenty of time for the cooking and sharing of high quality agricultural products, along with relaxed conversation. Some churches, she thinks, might even want to develop a program for teaching families how to reclaim the dinner hour as a graced time set apart from the chaos of the day. I think she has put her finger on a major issue. Not long ago Senior Pastor Glenn MacDonald of Zionsville Presbyterian Church took an impromptu poll among thirty-two members of a congregational youth group and discovered that only two regularly ate a family meal together once a week. To address this and similar situations the church has now instituted what it calls "Wednesdays Alive," an intergenerational evening of worship and teaching that begins with a common meal. Glenn says that he and congregational leaders found much inspiration in a saying that one member recalled from his upbringing in a Southern church: "Eat a lot together a lot, and good things will happen."

The Rev. Bill Greenlaw, Rector of Holy Apostles Church in Manhattan, where volunteers served 1,284 cafeteria-style lunches to unemployed or underemployed people on the day I visited, made a special point of telling me that even in this busy operation, those who dish out the food have learned to slow down the action enough for hosts and guests to make eye contact with one another and talk a bit to one another. Bill, a pioneer developer of meal ministries, emphasized that in his experience this kind of mutuality always proves absolutely essential to the affirming of everyone's dignity. In summary, Criterion One helps us to evaluate the "graciousness" of our meals and their ambience.

2) *Servers are led by the Spirit.* A second standard for measuring the missional qualities of our meals relates to the individuals who prepare them. It matters a great deal whether the actual serving of a meal is seen by guests as a personal offering of love from people moved by "righteousness, joy, and peace in the Holy Spirit"—or just

the opposite, a morsel falling from a master's table with little or no awareness on the host's part of others being present (Luke 16:19–22). To some degree, the welcoming quotient of congregational meals also depends on whether those who cook and serve them are truly representative of the church's membership or, by contrast, a small group of controlling hosts who jealously guard their status and keep their distance from the diners. Great things can happen when a good mixture of ages and sexes from a variety of socio-economic backgrounds learns to cooperate in ministries of the table. Carl Michaelis, who bears the august title of "Steward and Sacristan" at Christ Church Cathedral in Indianapolis, is responsible for preparing the numerous meals associated with the life of this busy congregation on Monument Circle at the very center of the city. Carl relies a great deal on volunteer help from members and friends of the cathedral and reports, with justifiable pride, that he has managed to "invite" several teenagers to join him in the kitchen, alongside older members of the church, some of whom serve as leaders of the vestry. Carl was too modest to say it, but I was struck during my recent visit by the way his commitment to excellence in meals served at the cathedral helps people of all sorts and conditions to perceive their holiness and join in their preparation. The creation of meals has itself become an attractive force.

Robbin Clark told me that at St. Mark's, Berkeley, she had witnessed remarkable exchanges among the diverse groups who came early to fix meals, as well as those who stayed afterward to wash dishes. For her parishioners, these became graced times for the honest sharing of spiritual concerns. For some, the common work of preparation and clean-up helped them to overcome their shyness and suspicion of others, which translated into their greater effectiveness as hosts. Indeed, she reported, a number of parishioners told her that they felt they had not become members of the church in the fullest sense until they had volunteered for table service at congregational meals. And that was especially true when the guests were mostly unknown to them. If we listen carefully to the personal testimonies of our volunteers at meals, we're likely to hear some amazing details of the Spirit's work in our community.

Dawn Ravella, director of outreach ministries at Madison Avenue Presbyterian Church in New York, told me that one of her highest

+ challenges /example HCC from service prog

priorities is helping people who volunteer for service in the church's feeding programs to see that these are spiritual events. Often, she said, beautiful stories of God's mercy and human reconciliation emerge from these meals. But then she and I agreed that we usually tend to forget these things, because we haven't developed adequate forums in the church's life for reporting them and giving thanks for them. I offer some thoughts on this problem in Chapter Five, where we'll address the issue of how our eucharistic services can center the other meals taking place in our congregations, particularly those associated with outreach ministries.

While full-spectrum participation by members in the production of church meals is a worthy goal, we should note that every congregation can boast of certain members with special *charisms* for overseeing the various meal operations. One leader I interviewed stressed the desirability of identifying the best cooks in every congregation, especially those with a talent for guiding others efficiently and graciously in communal efforts. My friend even came up with a title for these individuals. For her, the office of "congregational chef" ranks right alongside those held by others who have been appointed or elected to direct the church's life—like elders, members of the vestry or council, and chairs of standing committees.

Dennis Wheaton seems to me a stellar example of what one might do with this office. Dennis is a professional chef who owns and manages the Side Street Deli in Indianapolis. At the same time he and his wife, Cheryl, faithful members at Light of the World Church, a thriving Disciples of Christ congregation on the northern edge of the city, have entered into a partnership with their faith community that allows them some use of its large new kitchen for their catering business while they in turn supervise all meals associated with the church free-of-charge. In Dennis's view this win-win situation has resulted directly from God's guidance. Using the language of his African-American Pentecostal heritage, he says quite confidently that "the Holy Spirit has anointed me for a life of culinary ministry." Here is a perspective on vocation for all of us to contemplate, especially if we belong to mainline churches.

3) *Meal settings matter.* A third criterion for evaluating the quality of our meal-mission synergies has to do with perceptions of how a congregation's worship spaces and dining spaces relate to each other—or

don't. Here we may recall the great stewardship dinner that took place in the nave of St. James Church shortly after the congregation began worshiping again in its newly renovated sanctuary (see Chapter One). If we take a look at the earliest New Testament house churches, we find that this dual use of space is the normal situation. Those serving as hosts to Jesus' earliest disciples offered the dining chamber of their homes, sometimes with an adjoining atrium or garden, as the chief location for prayer, singing, almsgiving, and the sharing of goods—that is, for what we now call liturgy and outreach ministry. Most of this activity happened during and after eucharistic meals as people reclined on cushions or sat or moved about. Typical services of worship in homes during the New Testament period probably drew no more than thirty or forty,[4] which allowed for a good deal of group interaction.

Today most Christians in North America still belong to small churches. Quite a number of these start out by meeting in rented buildings with a few multipurpose rooms or just one large room that can be adapted to a variety of uses. When such churches find their membership growing, they don't typically follow the New Testament practice of establishing a parallel small group in a new location. Instead, they acquire property of their own and usually move quickly to build a sanctuary that will look different from other kinds of public spaces. I wonder what would happen if communities like these kept some of their old flexibility in their new structures, perhaps by designing worship spaces that easily convert to dining facilities, or by making it natural to move back and forth from sanctuary to food serving areas.

Many small congregations have been worshiping in traditional gothic churches or New England-style meeting houses for a long time. Often enough they are the remnants of old and distinguished churches that once had many members. Dean Richard Giles of the Episcopal Cathedral in Philadelphia has helped a number of such churches, first in England and now also in the U.S., to reconfigure their spaces so they can reach out more effectively to people in their neighborhoods. He calls this "re-pitching the tent," an image that comes from the tabernacle stories of the Old Testament, where the emphasis is on pilgrimage and an ability to adapt to the local environment. Giles also draws heavily on data from the New Testament, emphasizing that worship assemblies in this period usually took place not in temple-like structures but in homes around dinner tables. He observes, wryly:

As so often is the case, our relations in faith from other branches of Abraham's family put us Christians to shame. The Sikh gurdwara or gathering place in Huddersfield [England] has the whole ground floor given over to cooking and catering, with worship facilities upstairs; the sacred space rests physically on the kitchen. In this respect the Sikhs show the Christians (we who are supposed to be above all a table fellowship) the way, recalling us to our own tradition.[5]

I've never seen a two-story church like the gurdwara described by Giles, but perhaps we need such buildings at this juncture of our history—precisely for the sake of mission.

Those of us who belong to "normal" congregations of one hundred to two hundred members with long narrow naves and stationary pews have to use our imaginations to learn from the worship practices of the New Testament churches. Although our modern plants usually feature adequate space for meals in undercrofts or parish halls, these facilities nearly always feel less sacred than the sanctuary itself. Frequently they double as gymnasiums or theaters or classrooms. As such they're a little austere and generally lacking in good religious symbolism. The resident musical instrument, if any, tends to be an old piano rather than an organ. Moreover, the quantity and quality of sound in these rooms nearly always compares unfavorably with that of the main sanctuary. We find it difficult to be reverent at meals in such everyday spaces.

But here, too, the early Christian worship tradition offers us salutary guidance—as does the teaching of the Incarnation itself. The Bible makes clear that the God we worship delights in sanctifying ordinary, common things. Jesus gave particular attention to savoring God's presence in everyday table settings and even claimed to reveal that presence in his words and actions. We remember, for example, his words of assurance at table with the tax collector Zaccheus, his parable on forgiveness at a Sabbath meal with Simon the Pharisee after a "sinful" woman washes his feet with her hair, his teaching on choosing "the good part" when Martha complains that her sister Mary is not helping her to prepare and serve the food, his sayings about the bridegroom and the new wine of the kingdom at a feast in the home of his new disciple Levi. Built right into our religious heritage, it seems, is a strong mandate for expecting divine activity precisely in the midst of our daily eating and drinking. Here some readers may recall the lyrical words from Psalm 34: "O taste and see that the Lord is good" (34:8). Many scholars believe that the tasting referred to here was not strictly metaphorical but referred to real communal meals associated with sacrifices in the temple.

It isn't really hard to take steps that bring our dining spaces into a more friendly relationship with our worship spaces. Inexpensive upgrades of furniture in our church halls or the addition of a few candles can work wonders. Live or recorded music can accent the spiritual dimension of the dining experience, but only if it doesn't overpower the table talk. Some decent visual art on the walls can help too. Some readers will know (or recall) that biblical scenes of eating and drinking occur frequently on the walls of the Roman catacombs where Christians worshiped in hiding from the second through the fourth centuries.[6] From the time of Constantine onward pictures of meals have been popular in church buildings—and not always in the main worship spaces. Da Vinci's rendition of the Last Supper, more famous than ever because of its prominence in Dan Brown's novel, was commissioned for the wall of a convent refectory rather than a sanctuary. Today many dining halls of religious communities in North America are similarly adorned, with Jesus' self-revelation at Emmaus ("He was known to us in the breaking of the bread.") being a prominent theme. Mainline congregations have much to learn from the Catholic tradition when it comes to furnishing their eating spaces.

In this connection I can't help suggesting a personal favorite, a painting by the English artist Holman Hunt called *The Light of the World*. Hunt's work depicts not a meal as such but a standing Christ figure, magnificently clothed but also wearing a crown of thorns. In one hand he holds a lantern; with the other he knocks on the door of a cottage overgrown with vegetation. The door has no latch, so it can be opened only from the inside. The most direct biblical reference made by this painting is to a passage in John's gospel, where Jesus announces: "I am the light of the world. Whoever follows me will never walk in darkness" (8:12). But just as obvious to those who know the scriptures is an allusion to the third chapter of Revelation, where the risen Christ speaks these words to the church in Laodicea: "Listen! I am standing at the door, knocking; if you hear my voice and open the door, I will come in to you and eat with you, and you with me" (3:20). Since these words follow upon another word from Christ that is about repentance (3:19), we have to think of the meal Jesus offers in that vein, as something like what happened to Zaccheus or the two disciples on the road to Emmaus. It is the joyful exchanging of an old life for a new one.

For the artist, a major component of this repentance at table is enlightenment, which occurs when one opens the door of one's home (heart?) and comes face-to-face with Jesus. So the painting also points to 2 Corinthians 3:18, where Paul announces that "all of us, with unveiled faces, seeing the glory of the Lord as though reflected in a mirror [the painting itself?] are being transformed into the same image from one degree of glory to another." On many levels, then, this artwork prepares the viewer for life-changing meals with Jesus. To those who may object that all of this is too subtle for the dining areas and kitchens of our North American churches, I can only say let's try it anyway, or something like it from our vast treasure house of scripture-based Christian art. Or let's make use of faithful artists today who are creating new images from biblical texts.

There is no single "best way" of making good connections between our worship and dining spaces, but the configuration chosen by Holy Apostles Parish in Manhattan can stimulate our imaginations. This congregation enjoys a beautifully renovated traditional nave, complete with a tracker-action organ. It takes pride in its high Anglican liturgies and its well-trained choir. Still, except for Sundays, major festivals of the church year, and evening organ concerts that are open to the public, visitors entering this fine sanctuary will find it filled with round tables for the parish's Monday-through-Saturday lunch program. When guests from the street eat and drink there, they are literally "in church," surrounded by eucharistic symbolism. With its distinctive use of space, Holy Apostles is making a strong public statement about its faith and its mission. Most congregations will not want to adopt such a radical plan, but many variations on the theme are possible, with the goal being always to accent the holiness of meals associated with the church.

Some congregations highlight the connection between Sunday worship in the sanctuary and other community meals by setting up a coffee hour station in a back corner of the nave. This arrangement can help to remind people that our post-service sharing of food and drink does not mark the end of religious talk and action for the week but instead initiates taking our worship into everyday life. It is the first stage of going in peace to love and serve the Lord. At St. Peter's Lutheran Church, a rock-like structure built right into the base of the CitiGroup bank headquarters in New York City, large red folding doors behind the high altar separate the sanctuary from what the congregation calls its "living room." As the Sunday Eucharist nears its conclusion, the doors swing open, revealing coffee hour refreshments on tables. People move easily into this space, so that the service appears to continue. The coffee hour then evolves into a sit-down luncheon, a fairly elaborate meal that the parish considers integral to its self-presentation as a welcoming family in busy midtown Manhattan. Although visitors are greeted and a few announcements are made, the meal is not overtly "churchy." On the other hand, Associate Pastor Carol Fryer tells me that pastoral care consultations invariably develop from the table talk, so she feels very much on duty when she is present.

At St. Gregory Nyssen in San Francisco the link between Eucharist and coffee hour takes on an explicitly liturgical aspect, and a dramatic one at that. As soon as the service ends, urns containing a variety of soft drinks, along with platefuls of cheese, fruit, and sweets appear right on top of the cleared-off altar table. People mingle and enjoy their brunch in the same space where, a few minutes earlier, they received consecrated bread and wine. Having taken part in this unusual transition on a number of occasions, I've noticed that nearly always some members are moved to meet afterward for lunch or dinner to talk over the church's outreach activities. The dual use of the altar as sacred table and daily table seems to encourage a natural flow between worship and work.

Sometimes efforts to connect our worship space with our dining space can go a bit over the top. One rector of a large gothic-style church confided to me that he manages to remove a row or two of pews from the nave each year, replacing them with chairs in the style of European cathedrals. So far (he thinks) the parishioners who have noticed this transition are welcoming it as a sign of upward mobility. What the rector actually envisions, however, is a seating flexibility that will allow for setting up agape meals and eucharists right in the middle of the sanctuary. I wish I had thought to follow up my laughter at this subterfuge with a friendly suggestion that some public discussion of his goals might be a better way of following the Spirit's lead!

4) *Effective meals feature role reversals.* A fourth criterion for measuring the mission potential of our congregational meals focuses on role reversals. We have noted that in a number of New Testament stories people who initially come as guests end up exercising roles that are normally associated with hosts, and vice versa. In Luke's gospel, for example, Jesus often accepts dinner invitations, but on nearly all these occasions his very presence, which is frequently accompanied by prophetic words or actions, reveals some fresh view of God's kingdom to his hosts. In effect, Jesus becomes the host, opening up a doorway that lures his table companions into a new life. The meal stories from Jesus' ministry noted in connection with Criterion 3 come to mind here.

Analogous things happen in the Book of Acts when traveling apostles respond to invitations from those on the edge of faith, resulting in transformed lives for guests and hosts alike. The paradigmatic story here is Peter's visit to the home of the Gentile centurion Cornelius, a risky venture for an observant Jew due to the threat of contracting "uncleanness" from non-kosher food (Acts 10:14–26; 11:2–3). Very quickly, however, Peter the cautious guest becomes Peter the gospel preacher. Even as he speaks, the Holy Spirit falls upon all those assembled in Cornelius' house to hear him, convincing the astonished apostle that God not only wants Gentiles to believe in Jesus but also to associate with Jewish disciples on an everyday basis—even at meals! (Acts 10:44–48). Two conversions have occurred here: One involves the entire household of Cornelius, and the other happens to Peter and the small group of Jewish Christian guests accompanying him.

Where can we see role reversals and conversions taking place in our congregational meals? To answer this question we'll want to look not only at meals that intentionally reach beyond our church membership to serve our neighbors but also at in-house meals with less specific agendas, like Sunday evening dinners or picnics where both guests and hosts typically belong to our church community. Often unnoticed in this second kind of meal gathering are painful social and

economic inequities among members that work against our full communion with one another, both at table and in the work of the church.
Differences in the status of our members' physical health may also
create problems, in that some participants may not be able to delight
in the food and drink being served. Yet even here, if we're properly
attentive, we'll often experience the Spirit leading us into a blurring of
boundaries. Role reversals and the disclosure of special gifts in those
who may seem to be "lowly" will grant new power to our congregational missions.

Author-theologian Frederick Buechner makes good use of this
biblical data in his novels. I love the signature phrase that he puts into
the mouth of one prominent character, traveling evangelist and con
man Leo Bebb: "Here's to Jesus; here's to you." The words are a toast,
an opening liturgy intoned over wine-laced Tropicanas at a series of
fantastical public banquets that Bebb introduces on the campus of
Princeton University.[7] Are these meals just hippie love-ins of the late
'60s? Or are they authentic sacraments where sins are forgiven and
birth defects reversed? Or both? The reader of Buechner's novel *Love
Feast* is never quite sure. At the very end of the novel Bebb, who's on
the run from the IRS for filing phony tax returns, pulls off a last grand
stunt. He flies an ancient biplane a few hundred feet above a festive
University parade on Nassau Street. Streaming out from the tail of
the plane are two long pennants in tandem, "on one of them HERE'S
TO JESUS, on the other one HERE'S TO YOU."[8] At first everyone
laughs, but then they recoil in horror as the biplane bursts into flames
and crashes. No trace of Bebb's body is found. What's going on here?
Should we take this comic-tragic character as a Christ figure? Quite
possibly. In any event, Bebb's last will and testament makes a spectacular statement about the mystery of Jesus, meals, and Life. And it's
no small legacy.

Nor is it entirely fictional. A few summers ago I shared dinner
with a small group of people in the parish hall of St. Mark's Church,
Cheyenne, Wyoming, a congregation that has covenanted with religious groups across the country in an interfaith hospitality network.
A chief objective of this group is to identify families in need of emergency help with housing and/or jobs and refer them to churches that
can lend them basic support and counsel while they get back on

their feet.[9] In the wake of Hurricanes Katrina and Rita this kind of faith-based service is likely to grow exponentially across the U.S. and will surely become a basic feature of our national life for some time to come.

One popular format for getting the families and congregational helpers together is a weekly dinner. Technically, the families in need are the guests, since the dinners usually take place in church facilities or the homes of members and are furnished free of charge. Yet what I saw happening at St. Mark's shattered this stereotype, because the meal had been prepared by guests and hosts together. Later, when we cleaned up, the same kind of mutuality occurred. In fact, with no pre-planning, all operations quickly fell under the supervision of a guest, an unemployed chef who loved his vocation and wanted to thank his hosts with his talents as he waited for a job to open up. Throughout the evening I wondered where I belonged on the guest-host spectrum. I had come to Cheyenne as a visiting "expert" on biblical hospitality to speak to a group of clergy, but at this soul banquet I felt more like a learner than a teacher.

On occasion role reversals at our outreach meals will occur when those providing food and facilities take the additional step of opening themselves to the Spirit's guidance and offering up their need to control. By faith in that guidance we can sometimes get beyond seeing our host roles primarily as a good work that confirms our righteousness. Instead we can learn to be served by our guests, receiving the gifts they bear with joy and gratitude. Over time we can grow to expect the win-win situations that tend to disclose themselves at table while at the same time maturing in our ability to give thanks for them. The way forward here is contemplative prayer, which can't be manufactured on the spot but must be learned over time through disciplined practice. I made this discovery many years ago when I visited All Angels Church in New York to teach workers in the congregation's soup kitchen something about New Testament hospitality. I had planned to emphasize the role reversals that often take place between guests and hosts. Very quickly, however, I saw that they had already put into practice nearly everything I was about to say, because they had developed the habit of praying together at length before opening their doors to guests.

Here we may return to those congregational meals that are primarily for church members. Theoretically, all of us partake as equal disciples in these settings. Yet often that equality just doesn't exist. Despite our best efforts to achieve parity and mutuality—perhaps through the use of round tables—most of us can still tell which are the places of honor, and which are not. Jesus said: "When you are invited, go and sit down at the lowest place, so that when your host comes, he may say to you, 'Friend, move up higher'" (Luke 14:10). And Paul wrote: "I say to everyone among you not to think of yourself more highly than you ought to think" (Rom 12:3). I wonder what would happen at our church suppers if those occupying official leadership positions meditated on these passages, both of which occur in a eucharistic context. By doing so, they could perhaps work with the Spirit to draw out the gifts of table companions who do not (yet) receive much honor or responsibility in our communities (see 1 Corinthians 12:21–25).

After-church coffee hours provide a special case study of role reversals at a meal. In most congregations the task of setting up coffee hour refreshments rotates among the members, which means that many people feel some ownership of the process. On any given Sunday a large majority of the "guests" (many of whom also serve as hosts) hold membership in the church or attend services on a regular basis. But new people always show up as well: friends, relatives, and drop-ins, some of whom will be testing the waters to determine whether they want to move toward a more formal affiliation with our community.

In such a highly charged setting it's not uncommon for church members to extend a genuinely warm welcome to newcomers but then to leave them abruptly for others, with whom talk comes more easily. By contrast, it's also possible—and I've seen it many times—to smother strangers with attention, perhaps out of anxiety or a sense of duty. In her book *Entertaining Angels* Elizabeth Geitz calls this phenomenon "the attack of the killer-greeters."[10] When it happens, we don't really "receive" strangers, because they don't have the psychic space to speak freely. Henri Nouwen reminds us that in his native Dutch the word for hospitality is *gastvrijheid,* which literally means the "freedom of the guest."[11]

Somehow we need to develop a *via media* for our coffee hour hospitality that is guided by biblical stories like Abraham's welcoming of the three travelers (Gen 18). In his zeal to please, Abraham initially overwhelms them with food and drink, but because he also knows the

Bedouin tradition about guests as bearers of gifts, he is able to let go of his super-servant role long enough to hear the special message of good news that they have brought for him and Sarah. We all need to wear our host roles lightly.

On many occasions the new people at our coffee hours will come with gifts and talents that we desperately need, but sometimes they themselves will not become aware of their treasures until the Spirit brings them to light through conversation. Skillful hosts who believe that such revelations can actually occur in the sharing of food and drink will be able to facilitate them by shifting to the guest role. Often, however, we get stuck in the early stages of greeting newcomers, like dwelling on the things we have in common and keeping our talk on a happy note. If we stay on that level, we usually miss out on the more profound gifts from our guests that the scriptures promise.

A similar kind of stuckness can occur in our attempts to impress upon guests how special our congregation is. But unless we do this with faith in Christ's presence among us as ultimate host, we may fall into boasting about superficialities and forget our stories about the life-changing power of the gospel in our community. One thing is certain: Nearly all of those who show up at our post-service gatherings will be in need and on a pilgrimage—just as we are. This means that we hosts especially need to grow in our ability to listen creatively, a process that takes time and may require training by those with a *charisma* for discerning what happens beneath the surface during mealtime conversations. Some congregations might even want to appoint "deacons of the coffee hour," whose task would be to monitor the subtleties of this unique gathering, intervene now and then to encourage deeper forms of hospitality, and report back to other church members on the role reversals in which they have participated. Some form of this report might even find its way into our eucharistic services.

5) Meal outreach is a long-term project. A fifth marker for helping us recognize and realize the potential of our outreach through meals has to be applied over the long haul and with great care. This benchmark could be the most important one of all because it has to do with the generativity of our meals, with the attitudes and affections and events that emerge from them on a regular basis. Here we can't point to simple cause-effect relationships. Our meals aren't—or shouldn't *gleaning ministry*

Baltimore's example

Thanksgiving with Bea Gaddy

be—controlled scientific experiments, so their "outcomes" can't be precisely measured. Yet over time, we will be able to identify emerging patterns and trends of ministry in our congregational life that correlate directly with particular times of eating and drinking together.

We find a window on this process in the soup kitchen ministry at Holy Apostles Church, Manhattan. Since its founding in 1982, this now legendary feeding program (the largest of its kind in New York City) has continued to be the parish's chief form of outreach to its neighborhood. But many other ministries have grown up alongside it. This is how Associate Rector and Program Director Liz Maxwell describes the activities that now cluster around the daily lunches:

> We are involved in education and political advocacy to try to change the systems that allow hunger and homelessness to exist in the richest country in the world. Through our counseling and referrals program, we also work with people individually to try to help them find their way out of poverty and off the soup kitchen line. Housed in a construction trailer in the church's driveway, our counselors help people find shelter, a warm coat, a job, a detox program—and some hope that they matter and things can get better.[12]

These ministries all seem to be natural outgrowths of the soup kitchen ministry, but they didn't develop spontaneously. In fact, most of them evolved out of table conversations between guests and hosts. If we are open to the Spirit's guidance, church meals will generate new forms of mission even when they themselves are already missionary events.

What has come as something of a surprise to guests and hosts alike at Holy Apostles is the emergence of the Soup Kitchen Writers' Workshop, which recently celebrated its first decade of service. Liz Maxwell says this about it:

> Sometimes people ask me why we have a writing workshop in a soup kitchen. "Isn't this frivolous?" they say. "Shouldn't you be focusing on the basic human needs: food, clothing, shelter?" Over the years, I have come to respond that writing—telling one's story—is a basic human need. Writing is food for

*WATER, hunger
PRAYER*

the soul. . . . Writing—telling a story with heart and courage and the best skill a writer can muster—nourishes the one who tells it. [13]

Maxwell's comments occur in the foreward to an extraordinary book of compositions by soup kitchen guests that she edited with Susan Shapiro. It's called *Food for the Soul: Selections from the Holy Apostles Soup Kitchen Writers' Workshop.*

How did this come to be? The workshop was in fact the brainchild of a single individual, author Ian Frazier, who contributes regularly to *The New Yorker.* Having received a grant to set up an arts program with a nonprofit organization of his choice, he thought immediately of Holy Apostles. But why? A few words from his introduction to the book are revealing:

> All churches talk about Christ's teachings—here was a church that took his injunction about feeding the hungry and put it into practice on a big-city scale. I admired this enormously, and in the years in which I've come to know the church better my admiration has only increased. [14]

Frazier, who has never been a member of Holy Apostles, found himself so moved by the church's faith commitment to its table ministry that he quickly offered his treasure and talent to start up a different kind of feeding program alongside it, a companion ministry that would nourish the needs of the inner person.

It's a sign of the Spirit's guidance, I think, that this unique workshop has flourished for more than ten years now and has produced a book-length collection of poems and stories by guests at the soup kitchen, some of whom live hard lives on the street. Frazier notes toward the end of his Introduction that he initially underestimated the sheer quantity of suffering that many workshop participants were undergoing. Yet he adds: "I don't want to make light of these hardships . . . when I say that a main feature of the Writers' Workshop has been that it is fun . . . It's satisfying." [15] Yes, this makes good sense, because souls are being fed, and not least with "righteousness, peace, and joy in the Holy Spirit."

If we want to put a biblical name on the desired outcome of our meals, we need go no further than Paul's famous phrase "the fruit of the Spirit" (Gal 5:22). The Greek word Paul uses for "fruit" is *karpos*, a singular noun that emphasizes the organic unity of the Spirit's produce, even in its multiplicity. The virtues that the apostle associates with this fruit apply most naturally to everyday relationships in a community. They are "love, joy, peace, patience, kindness, generosity, faith, gentleness, self-control." At first glance, Paul's list appears to be a little "soft" and not ideally suited to mission work. Where are the more robust, outgoing virtues, like boldness and enthusiasm? I would answer—because I think Paul implies this throughout his writings— that the extraverted virtues, definitely needed for missionary outreach, often disclose themselves through the more spectacular charismatic gifts, but that these in turn tend to emerge with regularity only when our day-to-day fruit-bearing persists, quietly and over the long haul. The bottom line is that the fruit of the Spirit and the gifts of the Spirit are meant to cooperate lovingly with their own special synergy.

For Paul, community meals provide the optimum setting for this cooperation. We see that conviction expressed most clearly in 1 Corinthians 11–14, a lengthy discourse on the eucharistic supper at Corinth that accents the guiding role of love in the use of charismatic gifts (see 13:1–7). And, of course, we can also call once again on Romans 14:17, where the experience of righteousness, peace, and joy in the Holy Spirit is specifically linked to occasions of congregational eating and drinking.

How can we grow in our ability to discern the fruit of the Spirit in our meals, cultivating it so that it strengthens our congregation's outreach to others? One basic practice we'll want to adopt is paying close attention to the way gratitude, when expressed in conversations or prayers at table, often nudges us forward into ministries of peace and justice. It's been my experience that all gifts named and savored with thanksgiving in Christ's presence tend to move us toward new tasks in the world. So, even when tedious business lunches or tense, issue-oriented meetings with civic leaders over coffee and donuts threaten to numb our religious sensibilities, we can probably find things that we're genuinely grateful for and speak about them. If we do so, we're very likely to feel the movement of the Spirit, who knows

Praise God

no boundaries between secular and sacred and is always opening doors into partnerships with strangers for the sake of the kingdom (Acts 10).

Toward a Network of Synergies

Russell Chandler, a former religion editor for the *Los Angeles Times*, has written a whimsical but serious-minded book called *Feeding the Flock: Restaurants and Churches You'd Stand in Line For.*[16] Chandler makes the case that more similarities exist between religious communities and for-profit eating establishments than most of us think, particularly in the areas of self-presentation and management. He also thinks that church leaders can learn a good deal from studying these similarities. One point that caught my eye was the author's repeated use of the term "menu" in connection with congregational life. "The menu," he writes, "is the church's worship, witness, and work. . . . It's what enables the church's mission."[17] Chandler doesn't comment much on how actual congregational meals might appear on our menus, but the image he offers can stimulate our imaginations by helping us reflect on the ways we tell people (or neglect to tell them) what we're up to with the diverse meals of our community's life.

On one level, the issue has to do with advertising. Chandler suggests bulletins, high quality signage in and around the church, newsletters, and the like to display our menu of activities. But he also reminds us that word-of-mouth testimony from satisfied customers will prove to be the best sort of enticement, for churches as well as restaurants. Chandler's judgment might have to be modified a bit in this era of websites and e-mails, but the jury is still out on such matters. Personal words, face to face—and especially at table—carry great power. In any case, the deeper issue, I think, the one this book tries to address, is whether our meals, when viewed together, really help us to present our congregations as banquet communities that are celebrating the love of God in Christ and extending it to all. Do our meals, taken as a group, look and feel like soul banquets that not only nurture our own humanity but also overflow into our neighborhoods and the wider world? Do our eating and drinking events work together to satisfy those who "hunger and thirst after righteousness" (Matt 5:6)? Do gifts of the Spirit make their appearance at our tables, and in such a way that they combine with one another to empower special vocations within the *Missio Dei*? I wrote these words in early September, 2005, as New Orleans was still under water, and thousands were going hungry in all sorts of physical and spiritual ways. I wondered then if religious groups who already thought of themselves as banquet communities in their own locales would be among the first to help with this massive tragedy. It's too early to tell whether a positive correlation exists here, but anecdotal evidence from journals like *The Christian Century* and *Christianity Today* suggests it.

We have been using the term "synergy" to describe the foundational connection between meals and mission in the Judaeo-Christian tradition. At St. Paul's Chapel, Ground Zero, this synergy took the form of interplay between the ritual meal of the Eucharist and the church's emergency feeding program for workers, an interplay that energized many other outreach ministries. I'm convinced that an infinite number of variations on this theme can occur in our own congregations. But if this is to happen, we have to identify and monitor the whole circle of our meals, exploring their potential not only as individual events but also as a group.

Hence the phrase "network of synergies." Anyone who has ever gotten involved in a systems approach to organizational behavior[18] will know that the various meals of our congregation's life always serve to express the deeper structures and subconscious forces at work among us. Meals are one important window into our church system. In some cases particular meals will be labeled "dysfunctional," because they are symptoms of disorder rather than wholesome displays of evangelical outreach. Signs of disease and good health often will coexist, despite our best efforts, since human sinfulness never just goes away.

My purpose in using the word "network" is to state a goal. We want to move toward a consistency in our meal practices that can actually be seen and savored by those who come in contact with them. Networks can't simply do away with systems, which are basic animal things and have a tremendous capacity for self-preservation. But creating a network can change a system by opening up new channels of sensitivity to the Spirit's leading. Networks can provide structures of trust that promote wholeness and healing. The biblical words that come to mind here are "building up the body of Christ," a form of which Paul uses some nine times in his descriptions of church meals (Rom 14:19; 15:2; 1 Cor 10:23; 14:3, 4, 5, 12, 17, 26).

One way of helping people see our meals as a network is to introduce the concept to leaders representing diverse areas of the congregation's life, each of whom probably knows of meal practices within his or her own area of responsibility. Together, they may be able to sketch out a picture of how meals can work together in the church's self-presentation. Of course, an ideal setting for this discussion would be the table itself. A pastor I know on the West Coast has recently inaugurated an evening meal for church council members, followed by a short service of worship at the dinner table. Technically, the business portion of the meeting comes afterward, but in fact it really begins during dinner. "The new practice counters our tendency to deal with the church's life only on a nuts-and-bolts level," he once said to me. "Putting the table talk and worship together helps us celebrate something deeper, and we remind one another of why we are here in the first place. Actually the mealtime is almost a Eucharist in the sense that thanksgiving and mutual appreciation are the chief feeling tone. And this carries over into our debates about issues later on."

Creating a network of synergies in our church-related meals will always be a work in progress, requiring us to analyze many aspects of our congregational life simultaneously. It's no small effort. In addition, as all leaders know, each process that aims toward the deepening of our corporate life together will inevitably hit major snags. Meals will go wrong in both minor and major ways, resulting in injury to the entire network. If the sum total of wrongness accumulates without corrective interventions on our part, a time may come when the network of our congregational meals—including our Eucharists or Holy Communions—will begin to function as a turn-off to mission instead of an incitement. To forestall such a crisis, we need to be vigilant about flagging problems that threaten to undo the potential of our meals. Chapter Four is designed to guide us in our meal oversight responsibilities.

CHAPTER FOUR

What to Do When Meals Go Wrong

C hurch meals fail to reach their missionary potential in countless ways, some of them minor and easily remedied, some of them diabolically major. As we move along the spectrum of wrongness in this chapter, we'll do well to keep in mind the great truth that owning up to our faults as individuals or congregations is itself a sign of God's grace. Almost always it leads to the deeper experiences of grace that produce renewal and reconciliation. Jesus' parable of the lost son in Luke 15 shows us this progression. It's no accident that the story ends with a great banquet for the prodigal, albeit one that the elder brother might not attend—we are left hanging—because his crude sense of justice works against his ability to celebrate his brother's return. We'll have more to say about this troublesome dynamic later in the chapter.

From my reading of the biblical data and my interviews with church leaders, I've come up with three categories of problematic meals. We'll refer to them as meals that are a) capable of improvement; b) symptoms of dis-ease; and c) occasions for strife and division. In each category we'll cite examples and suggest possible corrections or changes of behavior that may be required if our meals are to play their optimum roles in the *Missio Dei*. We'll move from the least serious to the most serious cases. Our goal will be to do this not primarily as sociologists, psychologists, or organizational managers, but as practical theologians. Throughout the chapter we'll want to keep in mind the five benchmarks for meal measurement that we developed in Chapter Three (pp. 41–58).

Room for Improvement

My own experience with church meals leads me to conclude that most of the problematic ones in the circle of our congregational lives don't seriously hinder the spread of God's kingdom and will, in fact, further the kingdom's growth if we make some prayerful, practical adjustments. I think that's because wherever we proclaim the good news of Jesus Christ and genuinely try to live it out, however haltingly, God mercifully creates soul banquets to help us fulfill our mission. We are nurtured at Christ's table even as we are trying to figure out how to become better table servants.

When we look at meals that can be improved with relatively small efforts, we can think in terms of too little or too much. "It's a chef's worst nightmare," Emily Woods exclaimed. Emily is a professional chef who serves full time as a director of food services at a large protestant church in the Midwest where meals constitute a large segment of the congregation's outreach ministry. What Emily meant was that she sometimes doesn't know how many guests to expect at large functions, so she has to improvise at the last moment when the crowds swell. Not enough food—the worst possible situation at any banquet-like event, especially if it purports to symbolize God's kingdom abundance! At this point some cynic will surely note that Jesus fed the five thousand with a few morsels and ask why we can't expect such miracles in our own food preparation. My answer to that is the trenchant observation of C. S. Lewis that God usually acts by delegating normal powers to ordinary human beings—as in planning ahead. I would add to this that we should in fact expect miracles at table but that most of them will happen in our Spirit-led interaction with one another (see 1 Corinthians 11–14).

As Emily told her story, it was clear that no one person or group was at fault. Problems like the one she described crop up regularly in volunteer organizations where lines of communication and responsibility aren't always clear. Probably the best way to correct the matter is with a little restructuring that will allow the director of food services a greater voice in the main decision-making bodies of the church. If meals are really integral to a congregation's mission—a major thesis in this book—it's important for those charged with preparing and serving them to take an active part in the church's governance. Here I recall a conviction often expressed by Robbin Clark, rector of St. Mark's in Berkeley, that congregational chefs, even when they're not full-time church employees, rank right up there with members of the vestry or church council.

A second example of how church-related meals offer "too little" isn't so dramatic but may prove more serious over the longer term. I have in mind those eating and drinking events where participants offer only a tad of praise and thanksgiving. It's true, of course, that long, preachy prayers and speeches at meals can be downright alienating. They can definitely ruin our appetites! But we need to consider the alternative. If we don't acknowledge the gracious presence of God at our meals, both in our prayers and our table talk, we'll be unprepared for the discernment of Christ's body and exchange of spiritual gifts that have been chief distinguishing features of Christian gatherings at table ever since the New Testament era. If we miss this opportunity at our meals, not enough will happen to nurture our souls and empower us for mission. To be sure, we do customarily begin our church meals with short prayers, but what if these are perfunctory, or always "by the book," or unrelated to the particular circumstances of our dining together? What if it's always the same person (usually ordained) offering the prayers? And what if the prayers become signals to us that we can now put aside the religious stuff for the rest of the meal?

Several remedies for situations like these come to mind, all of which involve paying more attention to the inherent holiness of meals and committing ourselves more intentionally to full participation in them. One good solution, I think, would be a short, intergenerational course for clergy and lay people alike on the art of public prayer.[1] This would enlarge the number of people in a congregation who feel ready and able to initiate meals with a blessing. Prayers at table gatherings wouldn't be the only topic treated, but for most of us that opportunity comes up pretty frequently, especially at family gatherings. If families were able to take the course together, they might find help in reclaiming the dinner hour from all the forces that fragment their daily lives. Meals that are short on praise and thanksgiving could be enhanced with the regular use of short songs or hymns, or a blessing at the meal's conclusion that reflects what happened during the course of it. Whatever the approach, lay people will be encouraged to serve as worship leaders. Indeed, some of them will probably discover a special charism for exactly that sort of *diakonia*, a New Testament term for "service" or "ministry" that is often associated with meals.

As for expressions of praise, these may occur during the meal itself, whenever the Spirit moves us to speak. They need not be loud or long, and they could take the mundane form of announcing church activities that highlight our identity as the Body of Christ. In fact, anything that verbalizes our connection with the *Missio Dei*, along with a confession that God is actually present among us, qualifies as praise. Sometimes that praise will begin with the public recognition of brother and sister diners for the ministries they exercise in our community. Frequent honorings of God's work in one another, particularly at table, promote the growth of great expectations for our congregation's future. Additionally, these offerings of praise encourage the rest of us to search out and claim our own unique vocations. The bottom line is that praise and thanksgiving at meals can become the normal thing. But that said, we also have to be ready for surprises, because we simply can't anticipate how the Holy Spirit's manifestation "for the common good" (1 Cor 12:7) will be granted to particular diners on any given occasion. What an exciting prospect!

We can now move over to the "too much" side of the ledger, where the first example I want to cite, well known in church circles, is the frequent excess of food at our meals. This tends to happen a lot at potluck dinners and similar affairs where our surplus too often turns into waste. To prevent that, some congregations have developed ingenious methods for saving leftovers and using them on other occasions. Here, the caution would be not to dishonor guests, particularly those taking advantage of church feeding programs, by serving them low quality food. This outcome certainly isn't inevitable, since most congregations I know are blessed with creative cooks who do amazing things with leftovers. An alternative solution, especially in urban areas, is to donate unconsumed items from our congregational meals to organizations like Second Harvest, which redistribute them to the wider community. The point is that we'll want to deal responsibly with the excess when it occurs.

In addition, however, we need to look at the deeper issue of how our meals can symbolize abundance in a world where many are

— Mystic Muslim women's food practice

starving or going hungry. It's not that we shouldn't enjoy ourselves with excellent food and drink. Jesus seems to have loved feasting and was even accused of being a glutton and a drunkard (Matt 11:19; Luke 7:34). Surely he knew about poor people in his own neighborhood who got through the day with the barest of rations. Still, as Robbin Clark puts it, there's a fundamental difference between fine dining and self-indulgence, and we tend to cross that divide when our congregations have lots of good cooks and small groups who meet regularly for refreshments. On the one hand, missionary outreach activities that are linked with meals require an atmosphere of feasting, a sense among the participants that there's more than enough being offered for body and soul alike. On the other hand, such activities don't require huge amounts of gourmet food (the meals at St. Paul's, Ground Zero being a possible exception to this rule) or alcoholic drinks. Agape meals that feature simple but high quality fare like bread, cheese, fish, fruit, and vegetables can be very satisfying. But this kind of satisfaction—this feeling of our cup running over—results from combining food and drink with the prayers, songs, silences, and readings that are woven into the table talk. To this, we should once again add manifestations of the Spirit "for the common good."

Another type of excess that occurs in church-related meals has to do with agendas. Too often we impose our obsession with goals on our table gatherings. The sense of eating and drinking in Christ's presence gets pushed aside by our action planning, our impatience to get things done. Here we may be able to draw an important distinction between church meals and (most) business lunches. With the latter, food, drink, and conversation at table typically have value only to the extent that they move us toward the making of deals. Obviously there's something commendable about focusing on bottom lines, something that church leaders dare not ignore. But in the final analysis most church meals need to be more like worship services than business lunches. Even when task groups meet for food and drink in church circles, as they should, it's good to remember that our deeper agendas are subject to the Spirit's leading.

Some of the worst agendas that get linked to church meals are moralistic ones. They come in many forms, some explicit and many implicit, but they all send pretty much the same message to diners: "You are not worthy of eating and drinking here unless you are or do X,Y, Z, etc." Diverse expressions of "should," "must," and "ought" will dominate such meals. Jesus neutralized this sort of moralism by accepting invitations to eat not only with publicans and sinners but also with Pharisees. Paul wrote at length about how believers can never regard anyone as a second-class guest at the Lord's Supper (1 Cor 11:17–22; 12:14–26). Even so, we tend to sneak moralistic perceptions back into our congregational meals.

An especially poignant and ironic instance of this occurred as a movement in some mainline churches a couple of decades ago. The idea, reports Daniel Sack in his book *Whitebread Protestants,* was that effective responses to our over-consumption of food in a world filled with hungry and starving people could be taught through diets and meals. This was not a distinctively Christian notion,[2] but it was picked up by a number of mainline church leaders who called upon their people to avoid excess by serving food and drink that was *sufficient* for nourishment (a key concept). The recommended diets were planned to resemble the daily staples of Third World peoples, which meant that animal protein often dropped off the menu. Solidarity with the poor and starving was a major goal and led toward a revisioning of church meals. According to Sack, one Presbyterian author

> had particular advice for church socials. Threatening generations of tradition, she suggested giving children celery, fruit, banana bread, and fruit juice in place of cookies and Kool-Aid. In place of coffee and sweet rolls for their parents she offered raw vegetables, cheese and crackers, and herbal teas. For church social events . . . she recommended a "Stone Soup Night" . . . or a baked potato bar for Sunday after church. Instead of celebrations centered on abundance, "the most celebrative thing about a church meal is the people who are there. . . . The food . . . brings us together to enjoy our differences while affirming our unity."[3]

As in the case of business lunches, there are positive lessons to be learned here. It's absolutely true, I think, that we Western Christians need to reassess our beliefs about abundance and the ways we sometimes flaunt them in our consumption of food. But I'm not convinced that church meals themselves can bear the primary weight of this

This is about the goodness of the Lord, and

reevaluation. A few "demonstration" dinners might prove useful as teaching devices, but they need not be the norm. We are, after all, a banquet community.

Food moralism easily gets out of hand and picks away at the extravagant welcome that Jesus extends to each of us in every meal where his name is invoked.[4] No post-biblical writer puts the issue before us better than George Herbert in the famous poem that's usually called "Love III." There we find a believing soul who is overwhelmed by a personal invitation from Christ to dine with him. Recoiling from the invitation, the soul berates itself because it is "guilty of dust [mortality] and sin." More self-accusations follow, but each time Christ (named as "Love") counters them with assurances that he has taken care of all unworthiness through his suffering and death. Almost convinced, the soul proposes a bargain: It will attend the meal after all, provided that it comes as a humble table servant rather than a guest. But Herbert won't allow this "moral" solution. The poem comes to an abrupt end with a short command from Love that dissolves the soul's attempt to earn a place at the table. Only then does a transformation of behavior occur. "'You must sit down,' says Love, 'and taste my meat.' So I did sit and eat."[5] In effect, Christ is telling the soul that while he desires a closer communion with it, this can't happen on the basis of good deeds. Entering more fully into discipleship with him grows from more feasting on the bread of life. For us too, I think, sitting and tasting and seeing the goodness of the Lord, receiving it into ourselves, will need to be the first order of business at church meals. If we take this rule of faith to heart, we'll save ourselves a lot of trouble from moralistic agendas.

Two additional kinds of wrongness in our communities can create a negative synergy that prevents church meals from reaching their full missionary potential. The villains are competition and persistent worry, which tend to combine with each other not only during the preparation of meals but also during their consumption. Sometimes a kind of paralysis sets in that absolutely depletes our zeal for outreach. Of course, we need to remind ourselves that not all forms of competition produce negative results. In fact, competing can be playful and graceful even as it pushes us toward higher goals.[6] A friend of mine who pastors a small parish in Westchester County, ten or so

the Lord's peaceableness. (see p.67)

miles north of New York City, tells me that one of the real highlights each Sunday in his church is an elaborate sit-down lunch that follows the coffee hour after the 11 a.m. Eucharist. Church members, who mostly hail from island nations in the Caribbean, take turns creating the menus, which reflect their various ethnic origins. They also buy the food themselves and do all the preparation. It's their special gift to the parish, which has no budget for the meals. Everyone is welcome, and visitors frequently attend.

My friend worries a little that these festive meals might be getting to be more important than the Eucharist in the eyes of some—an issue we'll address in Chapter Five. But he's pleased with the joy expressed at the gatherings and the friendly banter about why one regional cuisine is better than another. He's noticed that these claims to superiority and put-downs of others are nearly always meant in jest and that the meals actually serve as a unifying force in his community. He also reports that visitors quickly catch on to this playfulness and get drawn into it.

Over the last few years, my pastor friend tells me, he's observed that when more affluent groups in the congregation host the meals, they aren't usually higher in quality than those produced by members of lesser means. He wondered about this for a while, hypothesizing that poorer members were making big sacrifices to keep up with the Joneses. But then he began to pick up little pieces of information in conversations that suggested a different scenario. What he learned was that money and help were circulating behind the scenes among the various ethnic groups. As a result, the so-called have-nots were receiving special support in their preparation of meals, and apparently without being shamed in the process. Here's a kind of "gospel equalization" that one can celebrate. But does it carry over from the Sunday meals to other aspects of church life? "Well, *sometimes*," says my friend. "At least it's a place to begin."

In dramatic contrast to this, we all know about competition at meals where claims to superiority and the diminishing of others inflict great pain. Often enough, those slinging the dirt aren't fully conscious of what they're doing. My experience has been that competition of this sort happens more often in table conversation than in the food preparation and serving. Some people simply talk too much as they eat and drink, especially about themselves. They become autocrats of the dinner table, consigning their less extroverted dining partners to prisons of silence—and thereby missing out on their gifts. For their part, the more introspective diners express their superiority by dismissing all table talk as banal and refusing to descend into it from their moral high ground. One can compete subtly as well as crudely for the best seat at the table. I suspect that Jesus' story about dinner guests rushing to choose the "places of honor" for themselves (Luke 14:7–11) applies to all forms of human pride in meal settings.

We could go on and on about this unfortunate tendency of ours. One remedy might involve introducing periods of contemplative silence into church meals to break up the competitive log-jams and open our consciousness more fully to the Spirit's leading. Then new lines of communication at the table would emerge, with different partners. Announcements about upcoming church activities might also prove helpful, especially when the future events have to do with mission and are likely to inspire widespread participation. But if interventions like these are to occur, designated leaders will have to take responsibility for monitoring (not censuring) the table talk, and they will need to exercise the gift of discernment.

I have a proposal for naming these leaders. It comes from the story of the wedding feast at Cana in John's gospel, when the waiters are commanded by Jesus to draw the water-become-wine out of large stone jars and take it to "the chief steward" (2:8). The Greek word for this title is *architriklinos* (arkeetreéklinos), which means a servant or friend of the host who is responsible for managing his or her banquet and may also act as a kind of toastmaster. This person has to make sure that the feast is really a feast, not only by keeping individual guests happy with food and drink but also by stimulating social interaction. I suggest taking the term metaphorically and applying it to designated church members who would pay special attention to the spiritual flow of our dining events—not seeking to control it, which is impossible, but doing what they can to encourage soul banquet behavior on the part of guests. Chief stewards in our congregations would be people eager to taste and share the excellent wine of the kingdom that Jesus is always surprising us with at our tables. Training will be required.

Another figure in the Cana wedding story from whom we can all learn is Mary, the mother of Jesus. Even in the face of a mild rebuke from her son when she complains to him about the wine running out ("Woman. . . . My hour has not yet come;" 2:4), she holds fast to her confidence that he will make things right at the feast ("His mother said to the servants, 'Do whatever he tells you;'" 2:5). The patient discerning of God's work at our meals on God's own timetable is an important mark of Christian discipleship. We need to remind ourselves of this when our planning for a meal goes awry, and we're about to panic.

Excessive worry, often in league with competition, can easily ruin our mealtimes. The classic New Testament story here is Luke's account of Martha and Mary when Jesus comes visiting (Luke 10:38–42). Martha's concern about food preparation is understandable, because she herself has welcomed to her home not only Jesus but also a group of his disciples—a real crowd. Preparing the refreshments, she quickly becomes "distracted by her many tasks." But what bothers her most is that she gets no help from her sister Mary, who is so enchanted by Jesus that she wants only to sit at his feet to hear his teachings. Martha naturally wishes to be noticed by Jesus and thanked for her hospitality, but when she complains about Mary's behavior, Jesus seems to make matters worse. "Martha, Martha," he tells her, "you are worried and distracted by many things; there is need of only one thing. Mary has chosen the better part, which will not be taken away from her" (Luke 10:41–42).

Interpreters debate about whether this text requires us to take Jesus' critique of Martha as a clear, either-or preference for Mary's version of discipleship. However we resolve this issue, a couple of points stand out clearly. The double address "Martha, Martha" is surely one of affection. And the "need of only one thing" is linked to the particular circumstances of this meal setting, which means that we should hesitate to make it a universal rule. In the end, what Jesus tells Martha turns out to be not much different from what Love tells the soul in Herbert's poem, although here it is spoken to a host. We could paraphrase Jesus' words like this: "Dearest Martha, let go of your efforts to prove your worthiness. And let go of invidious comparisons too, because they keep you from getting nurtured. Relax for a while. The meal, which I know will be great, can come later. For now, just sit and enjoy."

I can almost hear these words of protest from some readers: "Your paraphrase is nothing but romanticism. Relaxing doesn't work in a real church kitchen where things often get chaotic just before the meal. Besides, the people sitting at our church tables aren't Jesus. They expect their meals on time." True, alas—but only to a point. I'm convinced that we can, in fact, minimize the worries infesting our meals by helping food preparers and guests alike understand themselves as people entering into a grace-charged event where we all bring gifts to one another in the presence of God. No one group in the process is altogether responsible for the event's success or failure. A practical step here might be to gather guests and hosts alike just prior to the meal for a short prayer of thanksgiving that touches not only on the food itself but also on the preparers (who could be named), the diners, and the manifestations of the Spirit that will soon follow. The point is that throughout the mealtime period, including its preparation, we are all givers and receivers in the Body of Christ.

Paul David Lawson, rector of St. Savior's Church in Hermosa Beach, California and a specialist in family systems theory as it applies to congregations, tells me that over the years he's come to one major conclusion about what makes for good and bad meals. "It's pretty simple," he says. "Meals succeed when people don't give undue attention to food preparation and agendas. Anxiety, on the other hand, destroys meals." Anything we can do to defuse anxiety by way of courtesy, good will, and just slowing down the tempo a little will be a tremendous help.

Symptoms of Dis-ease

When we speak of anxiety, however, we open up a second perspective on how meals go wrong. Some have defined anxiety as a vague fear that floats about, pervading the whole atmosphere of our living spaces. That's because it can't be linked easily to a specific origin and faced head on. Often when we ask ourselves what we're anxious about, we can point to a few problems that vex us, but we know that our queasy feelings aren't exactly caused by any of them. Put another way, anxiety is a virus that gets into systems—family systems, church systems, corporate systems. The infection takes hold of everyone, though some individuals and groups feel the psychic pain of it more than others. Using a systems approach to congregational life usually entails measuring anxiety levels in our community as a whole, which in turn leads us to view "wrong" behaviors at table not so much as individual sins or poor planning but rather as symptoms of large-scale congregational conflict. A diagnosis like this makes particularly good sense when the same offensive behaviors turn up again and again at our meals, regardless of their special settings.

What are the most visible symptoms of dis-ease that we can identify as we try to understand our most problematic eating and drinking events? In his fine book, *Old Wine in New Skins*, Paul David Lawson uses family systems theory to explore a number of strategies that church members employ to deal with conflicts in their congregations. These include:

> *The forming of triangles, sometimes known as triangulation.* Here the geometrical term refers to two individuals or groups who, unwilling to face their conflicts openly, find ways of roping a third person/group into their relationship. The result is that this third takes on a heavy load of anxiety, transferred by the original couple.

> *Generational transmission.* This has to do with interpersonal problems that go unresolved for years and tend to be passed down as an inheritance from long-time members of congregations to those who have joined more recently. Usually the problems go unmentioned. They become the "elephant in the living room" that nobody talks about.

> *Projection.* A technical term in psychology, this word applies both to individuals and groups. The idea is that when we can't accept or even acknowledge unpleasant aspects of ourselves, we do what movie projectors do to film images—we make them appear on a screen. The screens are other people. They are the bad ones, not us, so they deserve all the blame and shame.

This is the barest outline of the diagnostic material provided by Lawson.[7] His book offers a much fuller, more nuanced picture of how our strategies for avoiding conflict affect congregational life. It should probably be required reading for leaders charged with monitoring the relationship between our meals and our mission.

Lawson doesn't treat meal settings as such in his study, but we can use our imaginations a bit to connect the dots he provides. To facilitate the process, I offer a few reflections on a recent conversation I was privileged to have with this priest-author. What I remember most clearly is Lawson's repeated insistence that it takes practice even to identify the destructive behaviors noted here, let alone reverse them. I think this is especially true of words and actions at table, which often occur with lightning speed and can easily go unnoticed as we're enjoying our food. If we decide to adopt a systems approach to our meals, we'll not only have to train our faculties to recognize the typical strategies for conflict-avoidance noted above, but we'll also have to work with our emotions so that we don't get all fogged over in our hearts and minds and sucked into what we're seeing. (Too much alcohol at meals accelerates this negative process.) In systems theory the technical term for finding the right psychic place to stand is "differentiation." This means that we're able to maintain boundaries between ourselves and the negativity we sense all around us. Lawson believes, rightly I think, that differentiation isn't just for professional therapists or organizational analysts or clergy. It's a goal for all of us.

But how do we get there? The subtitle of *Old Wine in New Skins* is *Centering Prayer and Systems Theory*, and it clearly represents the author's special angle on how we can grow in our ability to differentiate. According to Lawson, the best way forward for members of severely conflicted congregations is the serious practice of contemplation, one form of which has been winsomely described as "centering prayer" by the Benedictine monks Basil Pennington and Thomas Keating. Centering prayer is a modern adaptation of an ancient Christian devotional discipline and usually involves twenty-minute periods of deep silence. Many readers will already have some knowledge of it.[8] In centering prayer we employ no words except for an inner naming of God (usually with a term of affection like "Love" or "Mercy") that we use to "touch" words or images that come up in the psyche and threaten to undo our communion with the divine presence. The touching has to be repeated many times, and always gently. For large numbers of people, sitting for two twenty-minute prayer sessions each day produces

Centering Prayer

a growing sense of wholeness that not only reduces anxiety but also helps the practitioner stand apart from the conflict-avoidance behaviors that show up so frequently in our congregational systems.

All across the country these days, Catholics and Protestants (often crossing denominational lines) meet in small groups to do centering prayer together and talk about their experiences. I don't know how many of these groups, if any, link their practice specifically to congregational meals, but in the end it probably doesn't matter. If the net effect of the prayer meetings is to reduce anxiety and move toward differentiation, we can guess that every time they sit down to eat and drink with other members of their church and with visitors, their positive influence will be felt. On the one hand, they'll be better than most of us at neutralizing the bad vibes; on the other, they'll bring to the table concrete experiences of the peace that passes all understanding, plus a strong mandate for spreading it. Lawson himself believes that this sort of dynamic is at work in the congregations he knows. One thing he knows for sure, he told me with a chuckle, is that the centering prayer groups meeting in his parish haven't forgotten the vital connection between spiritual and physical nurture. Group members usually do their two twenty-minute prayer periods at a single meeting, but in between the two they take a break for coffee, tea, and cookies. Lawson calls it "half-time refreshments!" Is it too much to expect that centering prayer will attach itself to full meals of the church with some regularity?

In his book, *Unmasking the Powers,* Walter Wink offers a perspective on systemic dis-ease in church life that parallels Lawson's in many respects but differs from it in two significant ways. First, it relies more on biblical material than on contemporary understandings of systems theory. Second, it accents the role of prophecy in the diagnosis and healing of dis-ease.[9] Like Lawson, Wink doesn't make direct references to troubling behaviors at meals, but we can easily adapt his conclusions to the focus of our study, as we did with Lawson's work.

Wink begins his analysis of prophecy with a close look at the second and third chapters of John's Apocalypse, where we find oracles from the risen Christ to seven churches in Asia Minor (modern Turkey).[10] Most of these prophecies contain both good and bad news for the churches to which they are addressed, though two are mostly

commendations (Rev 2:8–11; 3:7–13) and two contain severe judg-
ments (Rev 3:1–6; 14–22). Some readers may recall Christ's fright-
ening message to the church in Laodicea: "I know your works; you
are neither cold nor hot. I wish that you were either cold or hot. So,
because you are lukewarm, and neither cold nor hot, I am about to spit
you out of my mouth" (Rev 3:15–16). Yet right after making this dire
threat, Christ goes on to counsel the Laodiceans in a loving manner,
assuring them that they can still hope for new life if they repent (see
Rev 3:17–19). In fact, every prophecy in Revelation 2–3 comes linked
with the expectation of a positive outcome.

As Wink explicates these paired chapters, he makes two observations that can help us find remedies for the dis-ease afflicting our
church meals. First, all the prophecies of Christ recorded by John conclude with the formulaic command: "Let anyone who has an ear listen
to what the Spirit is saying to the churches." This exhortation estab-
lishes that the words of Christ are also words of the Holy Spirit—the
same equation made in John's gospel when Jesus at the Last Supper
promises to send the Paraclete to speak his words (John 14:26;
16:12–15). Second, at the beginning of each prophecy John is bidden
to write what he hears to "the angel of the church" being addressed.

Here Wink launches into a long discussion. Why, he asks, must
the prophecies be sent to angels and not to the churches themselves?
And what, really, is an angel? Wink concludes that in this passage the
word "angel" probably denotes the collective animating spirit (small
s) of each congregation being addressed. It is something like a corporate soul. It can't be seen, although it expresses itself in communal
attitudes and behaviors that are visible. Most important, the angel of
a church can't be changed for the better through ordinary techniques
of organizational management. Replacing a "bad" human leader with
a "good" one doesn't go far enough. Restructuring won't help much
either, because the same spiritual agent remains in charge and resists
change with super-human power.[11]

I find myself dissenting somewhat from Wink's position at this
point, because I think that the author of Revelation considered angels
to be objectively real beings, guardians of local churches perhaps, but
not the same as the churches' inner selves. Still, Wink is on to something important when he posits that each congregation has a soul, a

spiritual center that must be addressed by Christ himself through the Spirit if real change is to occur.[12] I agree with Wink that the author of the Apocalypse has strong hopes for profound change and systemic healing in the churches to which he writes. He expects that the prophecies he copies down and sends to these communities will speak directly to their souls, which in turn means that repentance and conversion will be possible, even in the hardest cases. The seven prophecies close with a grand promise by Christ to the lukewarm Laodicean church: "I reprove and discipline those whom I love. Be earnest, therefore, and repent. Listen! I am standing at the door and knocking; if you hear my voice and open the door, I will come into you and eat with you and you with me" (3:19–20). We have encountered this passage before, in Holman Hunt's painting "The Light of the World."

Here, quite suddenly, a meal image takes center stage. Is it just accidental that a promise about dining with Christ functions as a climax to the oracles? I think not. We learn in the very first chapter of Revelation that John's vision of Christ and the prophecies accompanying it came to him "on the Lord's Day" (1:10), a phrase that names the time when his readers would have been celebrating their weekly eucharists. We shouldn't find this connection surprising, because both Paul in 1 Corinthians 11–14 and the author of the Fourth Gospel in John 14–17 assume that prophecies typically occur during community meals. John the exiled prophet can't be physically present in the churches to which he writes, but he can express solidarity with them in their worship at table as he narrates his experiences. He probably expects his book to be read in their services.[13] Revelation 3:20, which I take as a summary promise to all seven of the churches, could well be another eucharistic reference. In any event, it presupposes that those responding to Christ's words (his knocking at the door) will soon share a meal with him. The verse also invites comparison with Luke's story of Zaccheus. The rich tax collector responds positively when Jesus tells him he must "stay at" (read "eat and drink at") his house for the day.[14] Yet only when Zaccheus begins to feel that Jesus' presence is honoring his home, only when he senses that Jesus actually wants to break bread *with him*, can he repent and begin to make restitution for his unjust dealings. It's what Jesus does and says at his table that brings about this deep conversion.

But here we need to shift to our own day and ask whether these reflections on biblical texts can translate into guidance for helping us combat the systemic dis-ease that troubles our congregations. The answer is not clear. To suggest, as the New Testament writers appear to do, that we should expect this help in the form of oracular words bursting into our meal gatherings is a real stretch for most of us. Who among us would presume to pass themselves off as actual prophets? How could we tell if the words spoken were genuine messages from Jesus? The answer in both cases is that we won't know for sure, and this has led many contemporary leaders of the church to think that we should simply jettison this whole prophecy business, treating it as a cultural artifact from the first century that will cause more trouble than it's worth in our day.

And yet. . . . My guess is that prophecy is already happening at our tables: in the personal stories we tell of lives transformed by God; in short, powerful quotations from scripture that suddenly occur to someone and need to be shared on the spot; in seemingly casual exchanges between two guests where both discover that they are speaking to each other's deepest fears and hopes; in a Taizé chant that springs up out of nowhere; in spontaneous expressions of thanksgiving for gifts or people that no one has been thinking about but seem immensely important once they are named; and, yes, in unplanned words that a person feels impelled to deliver to the whole assembly at the risk of appearing utterly silly. These prophetic gifts come to us more regularly than we think as we gather for meals in our mainline and Catholic churches. Most of the messages, I think, will fall into two categories: calls for repentance when we have strayed from our mission and encouragements to continue with some challenging ministries—exactly the content of the prophecies spoken by Christ to John in the Apocalypse. Identifying messages as authentic won't be as hard as we think. Perhaps we can, after all, begin to see our meals as opportunities for hearing what the Spirit wants to tell our churches. If that happens, major changes in our systemic behaviors are likely to follow.

Occasions for Strife and Division

But real transformation doesn't usually take place without some blow-ups along the way, some major eruptions of the anger, envy, false pride, and despair that have been smoldering in the corners of our community life for a long time. Jesus pointed to exactly this phenomenon in his parable of the lost son (Luke 15:11–32). Almost certainly the elder son has been feeling for years that his father doesn't pay enough attention to his faithful labors. In his heart he has written the skewed history of injustice suffered that we call resentment. But only when his dissolute younger brother returns and receives honors at a grand banquet does he make bold to express his grievances openly. Why, he asks his father, should he be expected to *celebrate* this unjust favoritism? (Luke 15:29–30)

Church meals are full of dramas like this. For a thousand reasons people "take offense" because they feel that others are getting better treatment than they are. Sometimes, like the elder son, they put their resentment into words, which can actually be a very good thing, because then it can finally be addressed (see the father's loving words in Luke 15:31–32). Not infrequently such outbursts occur just before, during, or right after community meals, events that are intended to symbolize unity, equality, joy, and the like. We see this happening often in the lives of nuclear and extended families. Henri Nouwen writes:

> The table is the place of intimacy. Around the table we discover each other. . . . The table, too, is the place where distance is most painfully felt. It is the place where children feel the tension between the parents, where brothers and sisters express their anger and jealousies, where accusations are made, and where plates and cups become instruments of violence. Around the table, we know whether there is friendship and community or hatred and division.[15]

It's not hard to translate these words into descriptions of congregational dinners we have known.

Here's a real-life account of a family meal that can enlarge our understanding of church conflicts. The Rev. David Anderson, in the lead chapter of his book *Breakfast Epiphanies,* narrates a tortured table gathering that involved himself, his wife, and their two teenaged daughters. Right after the obligatory "Good mornings" came instant accusations from the parents: "Who has not changed the kitty litter?" "Who has not cleaned her room?"—plus at least three others, all in the space of eight minutes. From the daughters' side came protestations of innocence and unjust treatment. "Things got louder and louder," Anderson reports; ". . . a cereal box was slammed on the table. One daughter retreated into an eye-rolling 'I give up on this family.' The other ejected herself from the room. . . . We did not stand at the door and kiss as we always do. [My wife and I] sat at the table, and they left in contempt without closing the door behind them."[16]

Fortunately, a little soul-searching on the part of all four produced a reconciliation of sorts prior to the evening meal. Many families don't bounce back so quickly. That's particularly so in the complex family of the church, where we have no natural forums for reflecting on mealtime traumas and can't easily bring all the offended parties back together again for the airing of grievances in an atmosphere of love.

A story about strife over congregational meals narrated to me by a retired pastor friend would be comical if it weren't so tragic. The situation my friend came up against during the early years of her ministry was one in which just four people controlled the planning, preparation, and serving of most church meals. Everyone agreed that they were good at their work. They overlooked no detail. They served every meal on time and under budget. The downside was that many church members felt dominated and locked out of the host role. Their own culinary gifts weren't being used. There could be only four hosts, and everyone else was strictly a guest who had to play by their rules. Behind the small group's back, people started to call them "the four horsewomen of the Apocalypse" (see Revelation 6:1–8). Not surprisingly, the meals taking place in this congregation didn't feel gracious or inclusive. Over time, many members lost their taste for community meals altogether. Resentment continued to build, and nothing improved for years.

Paul was well acquainted with bitter, long-term conflicts over church meals. In Antioch, where he had ministered for some years, he confronted the visiting apostle Peter publicly because "until certain people came from James he used to eat with the Gentiles. But after they came he drew back and kept himself separate for fear of the circumcision faction" (Gal 2:12). The separation referred to here occurred in Paul's pastoral territory. Antioch was probably the first

Christian congregation where Jewish and Gentile believers participated in common meals as equals, with adjustments made to
honor Jewish sensitivities about kosher food. But even this carefully
thought out table communion proved too much for some conservative members of the Jerusalem church, and Peter was persuaded by
them that a "separate but equal" policy was more prudent.

Paul, incensed by what he regarded as backsliding, accused Peter
and the Jewish believers in Antioch of "not acting consistently with
the truth of the gospel" (Gal 2:14). For him, gathering at table was a
supreme symbol of how people shared (or didn't share) their life in
Christ. It looks as if Paul won the battle theologically, but not practically, which meant that he had to leave Antioch under pressure when
the majority of church members there decided against him. Most
interpreters think that Peter and Paul eventually got back on good
terms with each other. In fact, Peter eventually adopted something
close to the Pauline position, probably on the basis of his positive
experiences with Gentiles over the years . But this re-uniting of minds
and hearts took a long time.

Years after the Antioch incident Paul found himself once again
embroiled in a meal conflict that was producing a de facto split in
a congregation. This time the trouble occurred in Corinth, a mostly
Gentile church founded by Paul about 51 CE. The problem had to do
with wealthier members and their dependents, who arrived early for
the evening service of worship and consumed the best food at the full
meal during which the Lord's Supper was celebrated. The early birds
seem to have turned this ritual into a symposium-style banquet for
themselves, with wine flowing freely (1 Cor 11:21). Those who arrived
later, probably because they belonged to households governed by a
patriarch who decided when and where they could go out in public,
found themselves eating leftovers and consigned to the worst seats.
Perhaps they even missed out on portions of the Lord's Supper ritual.

Paul uses strong language to address the offenders, who may well
have thought that they were doing nothing wrong: "What! Do you
not have homes to eat and drink in? Or do you show contempt for the
church of God and humiliate those who have nothing?" (1 Cor 11:22).
Some kind of class and/or wealth discrimination is going on here,
and Paul will not put up with it. For him, the community meal, and

especially this Lord's Table, which memorializes the sacrificial death of Jesus, simply doesn't allow for second-class diners. All are equal in the sight of God, who bestows upon each a "manifestation of the Spirit for the common good" (12:7). Any failure to include the full congregation in its most important mode of gift exchange—meals—not only prevents mutual upbuilding but also stifles the community's ability to attract non-believers to the gospel. In the end, Paul's advice is simple and practical. Because all are infinitely valuable in God's eyes, those who come early (mostly the privileged by worldly standards) must postpone their feasting until everyone is present to take part (11:33).

African example (handwritten margin note)

We can probably imagine analogies to this situation in our own churches, especially when we pose questions like: Where are the socio-economic fault lines in our congregations? Do they show up at any of our church-related meals? Are they, in fact, reinforced by some of our meal practices? Do our divisions prevent us from experiencing our full giftedness? Our full potential for outreach ministry? What changes in our meal network need to occur to produce a more equitable participation? In short, how can we show that we have heard Paul's admonition to the Corinthians: "my brothers and sisters, when you come together to eat, wait for one another" (11:33)?

If we understand the words "wait for" not only in their strictly temporal sense but also in the sense of "look forward to the arrival of" or "honor the presence of," as I think we must,[17] then at some point in our efforts to resolve the conflicts plaguing our congregations, we'll need to make space for meals of reconciliation. These are magical events, true soul banquets, but they can't be simply engineered. Often they originate behind the scenes when just one or two brave people extend an invitation to others, whom they can hardly stand to be with, in the frail hope that God wants this meal to happen and will somehow bless it. In 1 Corinthians 11 Paul intends that the privileged will recognize how offensive their behavior has been to others and attempt to make amends with a new, more inclusive welcome. In other cases, the offended parties themselves may take the initiative as hosts. Paul tells the Romans: "If your enemies are hungry, feed them; if they are thirsty, give them something to drink; for by doing this you will heap burning coals on their heads" (12:20; see also Matt 18:15). The odd clause about burning coals (a direct quote from Proverbs 25:22) looks at first like a victim's attempt to impose a painful repentance on an enemy. But the context in Romans ("Beloved, never avenge yourselves" in 12:19 and "overcome evil with good" in 12:21) echoes Jesus' command to love our enemies (Matt 5:44 and Luke 6:35–36), so Paul probably employs even this metaphor of burning to symbolize kindness rather than revenge.[18]

I suspect that most of us aren't big-hearted enough to share a first meal with enemies without some negative feelings and mixed motives. I know I'm not. The point is that we just need to do it, trusting that God's compassion for everyone present will create the right atmosphere. I was delighted to read a few weeks ago in the *New York Times* that Pope Benedict XVI had invited the Swiss theologian Hans Küng to visit him at his summer residence, Castel Gandalfo. This was genuine news, for while the two men were friends in the 1960s when they taught together at the University of Tübingen—the older Küng having invited the younger Joseph Ratzinger to join him on the theological faculty—they later became estranged over issues of doctrine and practice. In fact, Cardinal Ratzinger seems to have played a major role in forcing Küng out of his position as a professor of theology at Tübingen. Yet Hans Küng accepted the new pope's invitation (I wonder what he felt!), and it was he, not Benedict, who briefed the press on the results of the meeting, which lasted five hours and involved a private dinner for just the two of them. According to the report in the *Times*, Küng took a low-key approach to the whole matter, noting that he and his old adversary hadn't resolved all their differences. But he repeatedly made the point that they now saw eye-to-eye on the major challenges facing the church, and they agreed to remain in communication.[19] Wherever we stand on the conservative-liberal spectrum, we almost have to say that the Holy Spirit was at work here.

Personally, I don't know of close parallels to the meeting at Castel Gandalfo that have taken place in congregational meals, though I suspect that a few readers have marvelous stories to tell about just this kind of thing. What I do know and continue to treasure is an exquisite film depicting a community's reconciliation at table. It's *Babette's Feast*, originally a short story by the Danish author Karen Blixen, writing under the name Isak Dinesen. Gabriel Axel created the screenplay and directed the film. Here's the basic plot line.[20]

The story centers on the conflicted life of a very pious religious community (probably Lutheran) located in a small fishing village on the bleak west coast of Jutland. The action takes place in the late nineteenth century, although there are flashbacks to mid-century. Two sisters, Martina and Philippa, are leading the community now that their father, the pastor-founder, has died. They have never married. Babette, the title character, is a French woman, a refugee from the revolution of 1871 in Paris that has claimed the lives of her husband and son. Mysteriously, she turns up one day in the village, having landed on the shore in a small boat. Penniless, she volunteers to cook and clean for the sisters in exchange for a place to stay. This arrangement goes on for years but seems on the verge of ending when Babette wins a French lottery worth ten thousand francs. The sisters are convinced that Babette will simply leave them, but she keeps quiet about her intentions, with one exception: She asks permission to share some of her good fortune with the community by cooking a meal for them on the birthday anniversary of their founder. The sisters agree but insist that the celebration should be nothing fancy. After all, austerity of life and service to the poor have always been the twin hallmarks of this community. Babette, however, simply ignores the sisters' directive, and we witness their growing horror as she goes about producing a full-fledged continental banquet—complete with soup made on the spot from a huge live tortoise! Martina and Philippa fear that a satanic sabbath is about to desecrate their home. But it's too late. Babette, who we later learn was a famous chef in Paris, has taken over the kitchen and enlisted several young people from the village to help her.

Terrified, the community gathers, nearly all of them elderly. They vow not to enjoy anything, lest they fall into the snares of the devil. They will simply comment on the weather, ignoring the food and drink. Among the diners, however, is one who doesn't know this strategy because he's a last-minute guest who's never belonged to the community. He is Lorens Lowenhielm, an old retired general. As a young cavalry officer he fell madly in love with Martina but couldn't win her hand because of her loyalty to her strict father. Furious, he left the village, committing himself totally to his military vocation. But now, after facing death many times over the years, he has mellowed. When he tastes the gourmet food and rare wine, he can't help praising them.

Ever so tentatively, a few members of the community begin to do the same, and soon nearly everyone is actually savoring the splendid cuisine. Partly under the influence of champagne, partly under the influence of grace, they start confessing their sins against their neighbors. Eventually everyone lets go of old hurts and self-righteous mindsets, asking forgiveness from those they have wronged in thought, word, and deed. And it happens! But even more surprises are in store. As the feasting winds down, Martina and Philippa learn from Babette that she has spent her entire ten thousand francs on the food and drink and won't leave the sisters after all because she's once again penniless. Babette is a Christ figure. She creates abundance and reconciliation by emptying herself. We can almost hear her telling the sisters: "And remember, I am with you always, to the end of the age" (Matt 28:20).

And still the magic of the feast persists. After the eating and drinking have finally concluded, General Lowenhielm. feels moved to rise from the table and deliver a short speech. Here's what he says:

> Mercy and truth have met together. Righteousness and bliss shall kiss each other. Man [*sic*] in his weakness and shortsightedness believes he must make choices in this life. He trembles at the risks he takes. We do know fear. But no. Our choice is of no importance. There comes a time when our eyes are opened. And we come to realize that mercy is infinite. We need only await it with confidence, and receive it with gratitude. Mercy imposes no conditions. And, lo! Everything we have chosen has been granted to us, and everything we have rejected has also been granted. Yes, we even get back what we rejected. For mercy and truth are met together; and righteousness and bliss shall kiss one another.

The words about mercy and truth and righteousness come directly from Psalm 85:10, as does the metaphor of kissing. In one of the movie's flashbacks we hear this very psalm verse climaxing a sermon by the pastor-founder, at which point we see young Lowenhielm storming out in anger, defeated by the preacher's hold on his beloved Martina. But now, at this feast, the biblical words lose their bitter irony and become beautiful to the old general. He takes them as his motto, exchanging a smile with Martina across the table. So, a final act of reconciliation concludes the meal.

Lowenhielm's words are a powerful example of what the New Testament means by prophecy. They are a special message from heaven for this little gathering, calling it back to its original mission as a community of good works that flow from God's abundance. We too can expect to hear and speak prophetic words like these, not only at the culmination of our eating and drinking but also right in the midst of meals gone wrong that are crying out for redemption.

CHAPTER FIVE

How the Eucharist Centers Our Meals

As far as I know, the meal depicted at the end of *Babette's Feast* is purely fictional. Yet it grips us powerfully because the words and deeds that we witness in the final scene around the table evoke memories of things that have actually happened to us—or longings for things that might happen. In either case, the film images linger and call us to reflect on their meaning. For me, one big question that keeps coming up has to do with how the magic of this feast originated. A major part of the answer, surely, is the sacrificial offering of Babette. She gives up her lottery money and puts her charismatic artistry as a chef to work for the little community. But another part of the answer to my question would have to be the risk taken by the villagers. They show up, dutifully, even though they are afraid. Out of politeness they partake of food and drink that they consider dangerous. But finally, as the general's speech makes clear, the strongest power at work in this soul banquet is divine mercy. Only the providence of God can bring righteousness and bliss together in a loving embrace. Just the right blend of divine and human activity occurs, and the meal becomes a transformative force.

Imagining an Active Eucharist

Christian faith holds that a similar conjoining of God's work with ours takes place in the Eucharist or Lord's Supper. Through the eucharistic elements, we say, Christ somehow communicates to us the inexhaustible mercy of God. Yet we humans also do a great deal at this meal. We create the ritual orders of service. We furnish the bread and wine and distribute it. We gather for praise, thanksgiving, remembering, eating, drinking, and much more. Still, we declare by faith that it is Christ who takes the major initiative at every Lord's Supper. He extends the grandest welcome and bestows the greatest gifts, starting with his own presence. He effects the transformation of our lives.

So goes the teaching that most of us have learned in one form or another. I wonder, though, how many of us in the mainline churches actually experience our services of Holy Communion as a transformative force. Often, I suspect, they're more like an obligation, a ceremony to be gotten through. Maybe they bore or anger us or don't seem real. I confess to having had all these feelings. Of course, mature believers of all ages have properly responded to such complaints by pointing out that feelings, while important, aren't the decisive element in the Eucharist. God acts forcefully, even if we don't notice it in our psyches or bodies. God's promises and Christ's command (1 Cor 11:24–25) make the meal sacramentally effective, and we receive its benefits by faith. I agree wholeheartedly with this position, which is held by most Catholic and Orthodox believers, as well as Protestants of many stripes.

But I also want us to reflect on important evidence from the New Testament that calls into question the status quo we often settle for today, which is—just *getting through* our eucharistic ceremonies as opposed to *entering through* them into the very presence of God with our body, mind, and spirit. To challenge our minimalism, I want us to propose the triple hypothesis that a) a lot more important things are happening at our eucharistic meals than we typically imagine; b) we can get more involved with them than we usually are; and c) our fuller participation in the eucharistic life of God will radiate out into other congregational meals, helping us to enhance their missionary potential.

However, before we review the biblical data that supports this hypothesis, we'll do well to elaborate a bit on the title of this chapter. If we're willing to imagine that the Eucharist is, or might become, a transformative force in our lives, then we can also treat it as the subject of a verb. That kind of figurative language may strike some readers as odd, but Christian thinkers have been using it for a long time—and precisely in a missionary sense. The most famous statement about the Eucharist as actor in recent years is probably Fr. Henri de Lubac's

SLOW FOOD and MISSION
Words, Water and Warming (Global W.)
and No Waste
Single Most Eff. Thing : Refusing Meat
UN Report - "Livestock's Long Shadow"

Effects of our food choices

bold claim that "The eucharist makes the church."[1] If I understand this theologian correctly, he means that worship at the Lord's Table is the *sine qua non* for building up and expanding the Body of Christ in the world. A large number of contemporary church leaders, particularly within the Catholic and Orthodox traditions, would take a similar position. As an Anglican, I can go along with de Lubac's formulation as long as we understand "eucharist" to include the proclaimed word in sermon or teaching.

This chapter deals with just one facet of the eucharistic creativity envisioned by de Lubac. What I'm proposing is that when we reflect on the reciprocal relationships that might exist between our services of Holy Communion and the other congregational meals we share, a good verb to use with the Eucharist as subject is "center."

Dictionary definitions of this transitive verb emphasize its gathering or collecting qualities. A centering force draws things from the periphery toward itself. In physics we use the word "centripetal" to describe this action. That is, objects on the circumference of a circle or the outside surface of a globe "seek" the center or tend toward it. I like to think of the daily meals celebrated by the earliest Jerusalem church in this vein. They displayed the community's joy and praise and generosity in a concentrated way, and so they attracted people from outside the group simply by virtue of their taking place (Acts 2:46–47). Today we can use the image of centripetal motion to explore the ways in which meal events linked to our congregational mission are drawn toward the Eucharist for their fuller meaning and power. I think the feeding program at St. Paul's, Ground Zero offers a fine example of that.

But there's another set of images associated with the verb "to center" that we might consider. One can center something by shaping it or modifying it, as in adjusting a lens or mirror so that it does its job just right. Here we may think of the Eucharist as a transformative force that moves outward, beyond its usual location in a Sunday morning service, to change things—specifically other meals. We could use the word "centrifugal" in this context, since it describes a power that causes objects to "flee" from a central core or motion. For example, a mechanical device called a centrifuge spins off gasses or liquids from solid substances placed inside it. But here we have to be careful, because the analogy doesn't work precisely. The Eucharist seems to act both as a centrifuge, a whirling motion that pushes things outward, and also as the things themselves, sacramental meanings and practices that are exported to other areas of congregational life. In the meantime, while all this is happening, the ritual meal on Sunday continues to draw people and events to itself. Ordinarily the laws of physics don't allow for a force to be both centripetal and centrifugal at the same time. But the gifts of the Spirit, revealing themselves in the Eucharist, produce exactly that kind of double force.

We can get a better sense of this paradox if we focus on ourselves as participants at the Lord's Supper. When we come to the sacrament, we do so as people already formed by all the other church-related meals we attend—and by much else. The fullness of our identity is what gets drawn into the Eucharist. That's centripetal force. At the same time, we are sent forth by the eucharistic ritual, newly empowered to shape other meals in its image. That's centrifugal force. In all of this the Spirit's goal is to choreograph a lively dance between the whole range of eating and drinking events that take place in our congregations and the one chief ritual meal of the Lord's Supper. As we get better at the dance steps, all our meals will move toward the fulfillment of their missionary potential. At their best they will become a network for the *Missio Dei* rather than just an expression of our congregational family system.

Later in this chapter, in sections entitled "Gifts Conferred by the Eucharist" and "Gifts Received by the Eucharist," we'll explore the reciprocal motions described by the verb "to center," giving examples from congregational life and offering guidelines for the renewal of our practices. But first, we'll revisit some biblical material, much of which we've touched on already in Chapters One and Two but haven't yet brought into direct conversation with the beliefs and practices prevailing in most of our local communities.

Light from the Earliest Churches

A good place to begin our review is with evidence that shows how one special meal, regularly celebrated as a ritual, quickly gained prominence in the New Testament churches. I see five probable sources for the earliest eucharistic liturgies: a) the ministry of Jesus, who spoke a lot about food and took part in many meals, often investing them with numinous qualities; b) the Last Supper, hosted by Jesus for a group of his disciples; c) meals with Jesus after the resurrection; d) the dramatic descent of the Holy Spirit on Pentecost; and e) Sabbath practices among Jesus' earliest followers.

Here's a short commentary on the role played by each of these events-clusters in the development of the Eucharist:

a) We've already noticed that Jesus often combined his sayings and acts with meal settings so as to reveal God's kingdom—that is, the expanding rule of God on earth. Jesus understands this reign as an unprecedented outreach of divine healing and forgiveness (see Chapter One). Everyone is invited, even the "unworthy." If I had to choose one scriptural passage that formed Jesus' personal sense of mission, it would be Isaiah 25:6. There the prophet hears God saying: "On this mountain [Zion, in Jerusalem] the Lord of hosts will make for all peoples a feast of rich food, a feast of well-aged wines, or rich food filled with marrow. . . ." For Jesus, it seems, this great banquet was beginning to happen, in partial and momentary ways, during his ministry.

b) The Last Supper, hosted by Jesus, was of a piece with the meals that preceded it, especially in its close connection with the coming kingdom, envisioned as a feast (Mark 14:25). On the other hand, this meal was unique, not only because of the provocative words Jesus spoke over the bread and wine but also because it occurred on the night of his arrest. The supper could never be remembered apart from reflections on the meaning of his death. Only in the accounts of *this* meal—and then only in Matthew, Mark, and Luke—does the pre-Easter Jesus explicitly invite others to share food and drink with him.

c) We find three stories in the New Testament of the risen Jesus revealing himself at a meal. They are the appearance to two disciples "in the breaking of bread," somewhere close to Emmaus; a dinner with a larger group of followers later that evening in Jerusalem; and a breakfast of fish prepared by Jesus for seven disciples on the shore of Lake Galilee. Two other appearances to disciples in an upper room, recorded in John 20, may have happened at table, but this is not certain. It's hard to judge whether the details in these stories are factual in our modern sense of the word. But memories of the risen Jesus eating and drinking with his followers on multiple occasions are assumed by Luke (Acts 1:1–3; 10:41), and this biblical writer in particular wants his readers to think of him as one who pays attention to historical accuracy (Luke 1:1ff.).

d) I understand the Pentecost story narrated in Acts 2 in a fairly literal manner. I think the Spirit's advent was dramatic and that it produced a radical change in consciousness and behavior among the Jerusalem disciples.[2] Their fearless public ministry of teaching, healing, and preaching aimed at conversion began at this time. The Spirit, quickly understood as an extraordinary gift from the risen Jesus himself (Acts 2:33), now became linked with the community's meals (2:38–42).

e) Sometime during the first two to five years of the Jerusalem church's corporate life, and possibly earlier, a decision was made by leaders to memorialize both the death and resurrection of Jesus in a single ritual meal held once a week.[3] Memories of the Last Supper had a good deal to do with shaping of the ritual, in part because the dominical words "Do this in remembrance of me" were associated with that meal (1 Cor 11:24–25). At first the event was probably called "the breaking of the bread" (1 Cor 10:16; Luke 24:30, 34; Acts 2:42). It's likely to have happened each Saturday evening after sundown (the beginning of Sunday in Jewish reckoning). Some scholars have called this an "extended Sabbath."[4] As a post-Pentecost meal celebrating Jesus' ministry, presence, and future coming, the earliest ritual in Jerusalem was characterized by regular manifestations of the Holy Spirit.[5] Paul's references to the Lord's Supper in Corinth (1 Cor 10–14) presuppose this sort of Jerusalem meal. The predominant mood of the eating and drinking, expressed in various forms, was one of thanksgiving (Acts 2:46–47; Rom 14:6; 1 Cor 11:24; 14:17ff.). Almost certainly, this accounts for the widespread use of the Greek term *eucharistia* to describe the meal in Christian literature from the late first century onward.

Two features of the earliest eucharistic meals stand out as being quite different from typical practice today in most of the established churches of North America. First, the ritual took place around a table at evening meals. These would have been more like our potluck dinners than our Sunday morning services. Second, the presence of God and Christ was frequently experienced through the agency of the Holy Spirit. Paul affirms that each participant at the supper is being "given the manifestation of the Spirit for the common good (1 Cor 12:7). Today, some charismatic churches incorporate this teaching into their celebrations of the Lord's Supper, but the vast majority of Catholic and Protestant churches in North America, including most of those identified as evangelical, do not.

Before deciding whether this is a good or a bad thing, we should go into a little more detail about what believers of the New Testament era meant by manifestations of the Spirit at the eucharist. For Paul, such revelations included tongues as a prayer language, healings, and "deeds of power" (1 Cor 12:28–30)—that is, fairly spectacular disclosures of the divine presence. Other gifts, however, were more subdued: words of knowledge or wisdom (1 Cor 12:8), teachings, leadership initiatives, and persistent acts of caring for the needy (Rom 12:6–8). Prophecy in Jesus' name was a gift to which all could aspire (1 Cor 14:1). Sometimes it came across as boldly oracular (1 Pet 4:11; John 14–17; Rev. 1–3).[6] At other times it occurred in low-key statements of exhortation and encouragement (1 Cor 14:3–5). By way of summary, we may say that worshipers at the Lord's Supper typically took active roles in the service, as the Spirit led them. A great deal of bodily movement occurred during the meal as believers reached out to one another to forgive and heal. In Paul's view, God's purpose in stirring up this eucharistic energy was, at one and the same time, to strengthen the baptized in their mutual ministries of building up the community and to attract outsiders (1 Cor 14:1–12, 16, 23–25). Almost from the beginning, the church's meal liturgy was understood to be a missionary event in both the centripetal and centrifugal sense.

Here we need to pause. Even as I'm now urging us to reclaim some key New Testament convictions and practices in the shaping of our contemporary Eucharists, I'm aware of how great the distance is from the first century to our own and of how uncomfortable some readers may be feeling about this reclamation project. I offer no easy solutions for either problem, because I don't start from the presupposition that the earliest versions of Christian faith and practice are necessarily better than later ones. Jesus promised—in a prophecy at table—that the Spirit of truth would guide us into "all the truth" (John 16:13). As far as I can tell, virtually all Christians, including those who deny it, hold to some form of progressive revelation. And that often means letting go of some things from the past.

On the other hand, having noted the widespread New Testament evidence for an intimate connection between the work of the Spirit and the worship of the people in celebrations of the eucharistic meal, we may at least want to consider modifying our contemporary rituals in the direction of ancient practice. If we don't, we could well be missing out on something that was once regarded as close to the heart of the faith, something powerful and joyful. I love the pithy admonition that one of my rabbi friends uses to counsel Jews who show an interest in expanding their religious practice but fear that the effort may prove too difficult for them. "Make a beginning," he says; "Just start and see what happens." I think we can apply this wise advice, *mutatis mutandis*, to the matter of the Eucharist.

I'm heartened by two pieces of evidence that I've come across recently—both of which surprised me. In his perceptive book, *Eating and Drinking at the Welcome Table*, Methodist pastor-theologian William McElvaney tells how he came to a new appreciation of the Eucharist midway through his forty-plus years as a full-time minister. He insists that his was not a movement toward "high church" ritual but a recovering of something the early apostolic church considered normative.[7] In part, McElvaney's change of mind came to consciousness through a series of informal polls he conducted with church members over the past decade on the question, "If you had to choose: sermon or sacrament?" Here are the results he reports:

> Almost without exception the eucharist has prevailed in people's choices, whether clergy or laity and regardless of gender.... What amazes me is the consistent choice of the Lord's Supper over preaching by group after group of United Methodists, as well as by a much more limited numerical sampling of Presbyterians.[8]

McElvaney emphasizes that he tried to present his question as a hypothetical one so that people wouldn't feel they actually had to rank sacrament over word, or vice versa. For him, the polls were mostly intended to test out some suspicions he had about the personal and corporate pieties of church members. He goes on to note how a large number of older people told him that early in their faith journeys they would have chosen preaching over the Eucharist but that in their fifth or sixth decades this original preference began to reverse itself.[9]

A related testimony comes from John Wilson, editor of the evangelical journal *Books and Culture*. Recently Wilson posted a book review on Beliefnet called "This is My Body: Is There a Eucharistic Revival Afoot?" In the review he offers this observation:

> Today, just beneath the surface, there is evidence aplenty of a deep hunger for a retrieval of the Eucharist. Within the last two years I have attended a number of "alternative" worship services, mostly arranged by young people, and in almost all of them [a] celebration of the Lord's Supper has been central. Perhaps these young people are rebelling against the marginalization of Real Presence that has taken place in the bosom of the church, just as Pentecostals rebelled against the marginalization of the Spirit.[10]

During a phone conversation Wilson later told me that in his view conservative megachurches, most of which celebrate the Lord's Supper infrequently or not at all in their Sunday assemblies, will soon be dealing with a rising tide of eucharistic expectations on the part of new members, and that this may well prompt some changes in their auditorium style of worship.[11]

I don't know whether these small pieces of data are at all representative of what's happening generally in the Protestant churches of North America. My guess is that they are. In the following two sections we'll explore this possibility by telling some stories about the Eucharist as a centering force and suggesting appropriate modifications of our own congregational practice.

Gifts Conferred by the Eucharist

We have been saying that the Eucharist exports itself to other church meals. In part, this means that we may expect to discern Christ's presence, the work of the Holy Spirit, and the advent of God's kingdom in those meals. And when we do, our words and acts of gratitude will multiply. How can that actually happen? Essential to the process, I think, will be the developing of a stronger intentionality on our part to understand how we and God "make" our communion together during the eucharistic service.[12] To do this, many of us will have to adopt some new practices. Here I'm not referring to anything arcane but rather to a threefold meditation that anyone can learn.

The first step involves allowing ourselves to enter into an expectant mode, so that we can be open to perceiving new things in the Eucharist we're about to celebrate. Prayer, a silent reading of scripture passages that will be used in the service, and a contemplative look at parts of the liturgy or order of service to be followed will prove helpful in this initial phase. This is, in fact, a form of centering prayer.

As for step two of our meditation, we do it in the midst of the service. That may sound impossible, but it's actually a skill acquired without great difficulty. It's mostly a matter of learning what to look for and then naming what we experience. Here's a short list of things that Christians through the centuries have seen, heard, felt, given, and received during the eucharist:

- the presence of Jesus, not only in the sharing of bread and wine, but also in one another as the Body of Christ assembled;
- a growing (or sudden) consciousness of specific gifts from the Spirit—in ourselves, our neighbors, and in our congregation as a whole;
- a powerful sense of calling, often in the form of a new certainty about how we as individuals and communities can use our distinctive gifts for the sake of others; this includes disclosures of what some Christians call "prayer burdens";
- repentance, forgiveness, and healing in many configurations;
- an uncanny harmony between what we hear (scripture, the sermon, hymns and other musical offerings) and our own self-presentation at the communion table or altar;
- honest and heartfelt thanksgiving;
- prophecy—that is, speaking God's word of encouragement or exhortation directly to one another's personal condition during the service (see 1 Corinthians 14:22–25);

- an entering into the eternal presence of God where conventional boundaries of time and space don't apply.

I know of no Christian for whom all these phenomena occur regularly at every eucharist. For most of us, just one will be enough to deal with on a conscious level.

Paul would probably sum up the points on our short list with his memorable phrase, "discerning the body" (1 Cor 11:29). For him, this is a holistic act that every worshiper, aided by the Spirit (1 Cor 2:9–16) and guided by agape love (1 Cor 13), can perform throughout the service. It is one facet of the Spirit's manifestation within each of us "for the common good" (1 Cor 12:7). Discernment, for the apostle, is a process that takes place over time when people eat and drink together at a real meal. It's not limited to short, silent confessions of faith in Jesus' real presence as we receive the consecrated bread and wine.[13] Taken together, Paul's views on the Eucharist constitute a major challenge to most of our contemporary liturgies, Catholic as well as Protestant.

The third and last step in the eucharistic meditation we've been describing is essentially a report, a prayerful, reflective accounting of what we've experienced at the Sunday service. Biographer Owen Chadwick notes that Archbishop of Canterbury Michael Ramsey once wrote to his aunt that after coming home from an early morning service of Holy Communion he felt he had not finished with it because it was "so big" and "many-sided."[14] Some readers have probably had similar feelings and, like Ramsey, needed some quiet time to process them. Eventually, however, our individual experiences at the Eucharist need to flow into our communal tradition so that they can define and fuel our congregation's missionary outreach. This sharing with others could happen in optional small groups that meet just after the Sunday morning coffee hour. The practice of mentally recording our "religious affections" (Jonathan Edwards) and then reporting on them in public will take some getting used to on the part of many American Christians, Catholics and Protestants alike. Patience, trust-building, and good leadership will be necessary. Keeping a journal will help some of us. In addition, we can learn valuable lessons from members of African-American churches, where testimonies come naturally, often during the service itself.

William McElvaney's account of a special moment in eucharistic worship gives us an example of experiences that might be shared in small groups. As president of the St. Paul School of Theology in Kansas City, McElvaney frequently attended chapel services on campus. He writes that on one Thursday

> I was sitting near the back of the chapel. The bread and chalice on the communion table were uncovered. The sermon by a student preacher came and went. As the time neared for the eucharistic liturgy, an unsettling yet compelling vision occurred. . . . The communion table with the elements became superimposed on my desk in the president's office, so that the two became one, inseparably joined, an organic fusion. The elements now, as it were, rested on top of my communion table/office desk-become-one.
>
> The bread and the chalice touched everything on my desk and everybody who entered the room. They touched the latest financial statement (which certainly needed something dramatic). They touched the inevitable government reports that gave administrators ulcers and/or the blahs. Nothing escaped the embrace of the bread and wine. . . . I don't know what else to say, except that I believe that after that experience I never administered the seminary in quite the same way. . . . What I sensed was an imprint, an embodied paradigm, a sign and seal of a deeper disclosure and discernment.[15]

As McElvaney himself admits, ordinary words quickly sputter out when we try to narrate an experience like this. One thing, however, is clear from his description: the Eucharist can break out of its time and place at a particular service of worship to sacramentalize other features of life. Using a term from our study, we can say that the Eucharist exports itself, revealing itself as a missionary force. Once we learn this lesson on a personal level, we become willing partners in the transferring of eucharistic gifts to all of our other church meals.

In her delightful book *eucharist with a small "e,"* Miriam Therese Winter tells a moving story of just such a transfer. It concerns the granting of a Doctor of Ministry degree to a prison chaplain. As a professor of liturgy, worship, and spirituality at the degree-granting institution (Hartford Seminary in Connecticut), Winter was appointed to confer the honor. Laurie, the degree recipient, chose the chapel of the correctional facility, where she often presided at worship, as the most appropriate place for the big event. Friends and family were present, and so were many inmates, pleased about the recognition being given to their chaplain's work. After the ceremony, refreshments were served. Originally this continuing celebration was to take place in the adjacent choir room, but as Winter reports:

> There were so many people, including members of the prison choir, that it just wouldn't work. I looked up at the communion table, and said to myself, what would Jesus do? Then I sent two of the women to bring in the cake. When I am old and feeble, I will close my eyes and remember the scene that sent shivers to my heart. The officers had lined up the inmates—we had decided to let them go first because they were the ones who needed the cake—and in a stereotypical communion line, they processed up the aisle and up the steps to the altar-like table, two by two, to receive on a napkin a hunk of cake and to snatch a can of soda from the bucket that stood on the floor. As the line moved forward, one of the women waiting in the pew touched my arm and said to me, "Isn't this eucharist with a small 'e', just like in your book?"[16]

And of course it was! Perhaps we could also say that the Eucharist with a big "E" was reaching out to sanctify this simple meal by means of its symbolism. But that could not have happened without the key decisions made by Winter, a Roman Catholic whose faith has been shaped by eucharistic celebrations since her childhood. The general rule, it seems, is that grace-filled convergences of God's activity and our own will create the right conditions for the Eucharist to do its transformative work.

A minister of the United Reformed Church in Wales, Peter Cruchley-Jones, has written extensively on the missionary dimensions of the Eucharist.[17] Serving full time as the minister of three small churches in a government-funded housing project called Ely (a section of inner-city

Cardiff), he has brought the eucharistic liturgy into settings that most people would consider distinctly non-liturgical. For Cruchley-Jones, the opening dialogue of the Holy Communion service has become particularly meaningful at church events taking place outside the sanctuary. In the worship book that he uses most often, the dialogue goes as follows—the response of the people appearing in bold type:

The Lord is here.
His Spirit is with us.
Lift up your hearts.
We lift them up to the Lord.
Let us give thanks to the Lord our God
It is right to give God thanks and praise.[18]

What caught my eye especially in Cruchley-Jones's reporting was the account he gave of an outreach ministry during which these eucharistic words were spoken. More precisely, it was a party following an annual Christmas nativity service that the churches of Ely sponsor for women and children seeking to escape incidents of household violence. The party occurred in a community refuge center where victims and potential victims had taken up residence. Here's how Cruchley-Jones describes the setting:

[W]e take food and presents to a very bare office room in one of Ely's hostels. One never knows if or how many women and children may come or how they may respond. There is considerable nervousness (on both sides) and the children are wary of men. . . . It is simultaneously deeply harrowing and moving. . . .[19]

Obviously, praying the eucharistic dialogue in this situation can't fix everything. The violence—perpetrated, threatened, and feared—still hangs in the air. Yet something is added: an almost defiant insistence on the presence of Jesus, a victim of violence himself who returns from the dead to offer victorious life. People who hear that good news can, in fact, lift up their hearts and give thanks—no matter what. Cruchley-Jones doesn't say so, but we may guess that some of those who show up for the service recognize the dialogue as eucharistic language and feel themselves unusually blessed in their sharing of Christmas refreshments.

Peter Cruchley-Jones has made a conscious effort to facilitate the exporting of the Eucharist to other church events. If we want to receive a full measure of the gifts that Holy Communion can bestow on our congregational meals, we'll do well to follow his example. One practical way forward is to schedule services of communion back-to-back with other congregational meals. Unless I'm badly mistaken, a trend in this direction is already developing in a number of North American churches. My own home parish, St. George's in Rumson, New Jersey, offers frequent mid-week suppers that follow upon simple celebrations of the Eucharist. I know this to be true of several other churches in the Episcopal Diocese of New Jersey, and in at least one case the sit-down meal doubles as a feeding program for needy people in the area. The now legendary stewardship banquet at St. James Church, Manhattan, (see Chapter One), was itself preceded by a quiet Eucharist. Everyone was invited, but most of those attending turned out to be people who were charged with responsibilities for preparing the event and felt the need to be consecrated for their tasks. The "missionary lunch" following the Sunday Eucharist at Trinity Cathedral, San Jose, also comes to mind (see Chapter Two).

An unusually effective pairing of the Eucharist with a full meal takes place each Friday morning at the Anglican Monastery and Retreat Center of the Holy Cross atop Mt. Calvary in Santa Barbara, California. The service is known to many in the city, and everyone is invited. Driving up the curvy mountain road can be daunting, especially in the early morning fog, but a group of fifteen to thirty worshipers generally makes the ascent on time. The composition of the congregation varies a good deal from week to week. A number of those who attend are seekers or marginal members of local churches. Maybe it's the gorgeous view from the mountain at sunrise that draws them, or the homily, which is created by the whole community as it reflects together on the scripture readings. Maybe it's the deep commitment to holiness that one senses in the monks, or the generous breakfast of natural foods that follows the service. Maybe it's even the Eucharist per se! God knows, we are all creatures of mixed motivations. In any event, the breakfast has always been a joyful experience for me, and also one at which I feel freed up to talk over deep issues of faith, doubt, and suffering with my tablemates. I've since learned that many others feel the same way. Brother Robert Sevensky, prior of the monastery, tells me that spiritual direction relationships often begin at this breakfast and at other meals hosted by the Holy Cross brothers for retreat groups. On Mt. Calvary no breaking of the bread or gathering around the communal coffee urn escapes the centrifugal force of the Eucharist.

To summarize, we can say that there's a good deal of contemporary data pointing to an expansion of the Eucharist into other congregational meals. This doesn't mean that they just get taken over by the Eucharist, thus losing their distinctive character as picnics, lunches for homeless people, coffee hours, and the like. Instead, they become more of what they're intended to be: the work (and play!) of the Lord for the sake of the world, into which we are called as partners.

We sacramentalize our "ordinary" meals when we find in them and bring to them what we've already come to know, more intensively, at the Eucharist. The optimum result is that in all of our community meals we grow to expect the presence and activity of the whole Trinity, especially through manifestations of the Spirit. We take on the practice of discerning Christ's Body as a normal part of eating and drinking together in his name. (Perhaps we'll even experience prophecy!) And we will give thanks at a deeper, truer level than ever before. In a groundbreaking book called *Worship and Mission*, originally published in 1966, Anglican priest-professor J. G. Davies pointed specifically to the Eucharist when he wrote that "the goal of mission can indeed be defined as the increase of thanksgiving."[20] Of course we'll want to add that there's a lot more to be said about mission, but Davies was right, I think, in naming thanks as the heartbeat of all outreach activities. Our various congregational meals will be most recognizable as soul banquets when authentic expressions of gratitude to God abound.

Gifts Received by the Eucharist

Not only does the Eucharist expand and export itself (thus multiplying the giving of thanks). It also opens itself up to the total life experiences of worshipers who attend it and draws them into its liturgy (thus multi-plying the giving of thanks). Here we focus on the centripetal action of the Eucharist, asking ourselves how everything we bring to the ritual from other meals might affect our participation. My guess is that we're not usually meditating on *other meals* when we approach the altar/communion table or receive the consecrated bread and wine in our seats. We want to meet Jesus at *this* meal, meager as it is, and mostly we want our companionship with him to be about liberation from our burdens of guilt and illness and worry and doubt. That's as it should be. A self-offering or "living sacrifice" of this sort (Rom 12:1) is often the most authentic thing we can do in worship. God welcomes whatever we offer, while at the same time renewing our minds (Rom 12:2) so that we can sense divine power working through our weaknesses (2 Cor 12:9–10).[21]

But exactly here, as God's power and our weakness intersect at the Lord's Table, we often experience something that transcends our need. Paul says that in the eucharistic celebration we undergo a transformation of our senses so that we can "discern what is the will of God—what is good and acceptable and perfect" (Rom 12:2). Once again, the potent word "discern" turns up, the very word we've learned to associate with identifying and claiming gifts for mutual ministry at every meal blessed by the name of Jesus. If we've tasted the richness of the Spirit at such "ordinary" meals, we'll probably find that reflecting on one or more of them during eucharistic worship will tend to be the norm rather than the exception. In fact, our experiences of personal and corporate renewal at these other table events can become a fundamental feature of our self-offering.

Unfortunately, most of our eucharistic rituals today don't accommodate themselves to the public sharing of such offerings. In the interest of decorum we are asked to keep our thoughts and feelings to ourselves. Spontaneous forms of communication with our neighbors in the liturgical space bounded by the eucharistic prayer and the very short moments of eating and drinking are usually considered to be in bad taste. "Table talk" is not an expression that we typically associate with our worship. True, a remnant of this occurs in some congregations at the passing of the Peace just prior to the opening eucharistic dialogue ("The Lord be with you. . . . And also with you."). But apart from that, verbal interaction among the worshipers hardly exists, the assumption apparently being that each individual must concentrate (hard) on making his or her private communion.

Should we do anything about this state of affairs? It seems unwise to push for major changes in our familiar eucharistic liturgies, since the spiritual wisdom of many centuries resides in them. On the other hand, one can interpret them, adapt them to new situations, and add things to them, as the church has been doing from its very inception. In fact, such enhancements are likely to happen more or less on their own when we begin to visualize the Eucharist as a Spirit-led event that welcomes people being shaped by their participation in a rich variety of other meals. Here are a few changes that might occur in our eucharistic celebrations if we choose to follow this vision:

- A close connection with a sit-down meal could become more frequent—either an agape meal that develops into a Eucharist or a meal following the Eucharist that encourages a continuation of it into everyday life.
- Sanctuaries may be arranged so that we can see the faces of our sister and brother worshipers as they make their communions. Passing the bread and wine to one another in a circle is one way to accomplish this. *Or throughout the service — Passing the Peace* *Choir? Prayers*
- A longer time span for our individual communions might be introduced. In most cases this would be silent time, but the Spirit could also inspire audible prayers and prophecies (see 1Timothy 3:14).
- During our personal communions, or at a time close to them, the laying on of hands for healing or commissioning to new ministries may occur. *This happens at Messiah*
- Eucharistic prayers could become more flexible so that they are capable of incorporating references to other congregational meals and the ministries associated with them. Precisely at the Lord's Table, it's appropriate to present ourselves as banquet communities in mission. To facilitate this self-offering, celebrants might invite on-the-spot contributions to the eucharistic prayer from worshipers. This would be a time to expect prophesies.[22]

-BIHN
-CSA
-Lenten meals
-potlucks after the service

Given what we now know about the earliest forms of eucharistic worship in the New Testament churches, these proposals are far from radical. In fact, a number of readers will already have encountered some of them, especially at mid-week services or week-end retreats. But even where that is so, we can almost certainly reap more benefits from our practice. In each case the goal would be to encourage manifestations of the Spirit "for the common good," which always means both community building and missionary outreach beyond our communities.

Can we identify groups of Christians who are taking the centripetal force of the Eucharist seriously in their liturgical worship? We can. One such community is led by Dean Richard Giles at the Philadelphia (Episcopal) Cathedral. He recently told me about a version of the Holy Communion called a "St. Jude's Mass" that he and his congregation, which includes many university students, had celebrated in the cathedral undercroft. The name of the eucharistic order derives from St. Jude's reputation as the patron saint of desperate people.

As people entered the worship space they found it illumined only by candles that had been placed at several small tables. Popular music played in the background. "We made it look pretty much like a nightclub," Richard said. Most worshipers were a little confused and didn't know what to expect because no leader appeared, and the prayer book language of the Eucharist wasn't forthcoming. So people just waited and talked, somewhat nervously. Eventually their chatter was interrupted by a series of "visitors;" in reality they were trained actors, but only a few knew this or suspected it. One of the newcomers posed as a drug addict, and another presented himself as a street man in smelly clothes who had brought along all his worldly possessions in plastic bags. All the visitors stood and talked about how hard life was. In various ways they all expressed a wish that they might become part of the "normal" group sitting at the tables. Some worshipers felt uneasy about this, but all tried their best to be welcoming. Most visitors accepted the proffered hospitality and sat down.

Then, as the growing congregation began to resemble all sorts and conditions of humanity, a designated leader stood and asked people to bring their tables together to form a single big one. When that was done and everyone had found a seat around it, the Holy Communion liturgy began. Richard recounted how on that night the eucharistic prayer was offered extemporaneously so as to reflect what was taking place at the gathering. The prayer concluded with a toast to Jesus, the kind one might make at a wedding feast. After the benediction and a period of silence, most people stayed and talked for an hour or so about what the service had meant to them. When they guessed or were told that the visitors were actors, they all said that the deception had been worthwhile because of what they had learned.

Despite being staged, this Eucharist apparently succeeded in highlighting the "threshold" character of every communion service, whereby everyday experiences are drawn into ritual space and consecrated so that praise, thanksgiving, and mission can emerge from real life. An important learning was that this seems to happen most effectively when the forms of our eucharistic celebration are modified in course by our self-offerings. Miriam Therese Winter thinks along such lines when she writes:

> Some of my most memorable meals took place in makeshift refugee camps far away from home. I came face-to-face with famine that summer in Ethiopia, and before that, in the sprawling camps along the Thai-Cambodian border among traumatized survivors of the Pol Pot regime. I learned what it means to be hungry, really and truly hungry, and what a significant blessing it is when that hunger is assuaged. After those searing experiences, the Eucharist, for me, has never been the same. I came to realize that Eucharist is at the very core of life whenever it is happening and reveals itself in our efforts to attend to another's needs.[23]

Here Winter's main purpose is to accent the eucharistic character of all meals that serve to address the real hungers of desperate people. But as a Christian professor of liturgy she inevitably brings all her meal experiences into contact with the formal Sunday Eucharist and discovers as she worships that the ancient service has been forever changed. It seems to me that exactly this re-visioning of the eucharistic ritual needs to be happening for all of us on a regular basis. It's built right into the transformation and renewal of mind (read: "repentance") that Paul expects when he urges us to present our entire personhood at the Lord's Table (Rom 12:1–2). So, for example, when we come to the Eucharist acutely aware of great deprivations being suffered

how
?

by our neighbors (as we did during the Hurricane Katrina crisis), why shouldn't we give voice to our empathy and our plans for help within the meal portion of our liturgies and not just in the prayers of the people?

The Maundy Thursday communion service at the Philadelphia Cathedral (imported from England) offers us yet another insight into the centripetal power of the Eucharist. Here liturgical architecture plays a decisive role. When people enter the nave of the church, they find no lines of pews and no altar at the far end of the room. Instead, worshipers are met by a huge rectangular table, perhaps thirty feet in length, at the very center of the worship space. The table is spread with a simple white cloth but is otherwise unadorned. All around it chairs have been placed, about ten feet back. When worshipers take these seats, they can see one another across the table, as they would at a dinner party.

Like a number of other contemporary services held on Maundy Thursday, this one incorporates a modified form of the Jewish Passover seder. However, unlike all other such liturgies that I'm familiar with, this one calls for people to come forward from their seats to the table, simultaneously, to partake of lamb, bitter herbs, and unleavened bread while the Passover story is read aloud from Exodus. Everyone eats standing up because, as the liturgy puts it: "Our ancestors were ready to go that night." After the Passover food is eaten, all return to their seats for reflection, with music in the background. Then the traditional footwashing takes place—around the table, just as the biblical story in John 13 describes it. A period of hymn singing and reflection follows. Finally, the service evolves into a Eucharist, with the chief prayer being offered antiphonally by laypeople as well as clergy. Then, paralleling the action in the Passover segment of the liturgy, worshipers come forward once again to stand at the table together as they eat and drink the consecrated elements. The service concludes on a note of high expectation. In communion with ancient Israel, the guests understand themselves as people ready to depart on a great journey, but now with a new kind of cleansing and nourishment to empower them.

What strikes me as particularly effective about this service is the table symbolism it employs. Almost everything happens with refer- ence to this very large object, smaller versions of which we all see and use each day. Although the worshipers don't speak informally to one another during the service as they would at ordinary dinners, they still communicate a good deal—both around and across the table—with facial expressions, gestures, and touches. It's a fine setting for discerning the Body. And as this process goes forward, people also begin to sense how the tables of their everyday lives are being honored and consecrated. Here the centripetal force of the Eucharist works together with its centrifugal force. Yet we should hasten to add that this doesn't typically occur without human creativity and effort. Someone must set the table. Someone must help the participants enter into the novelties of the service.

On occasion, we can get a better sense of how the centripetal and centrifugal forces of the Eucharist cooperate by moving our liturgies away from the physical structure of a church building into settings that we'd ordinarily call secular. Lyndon Harris reports that soon after the 9/11 attacks, leaders at St. Paul's Chapel elected to set up a crude altar table right on the edge of the dreadful Pit, the mass of smoking wreckage from which recovery workers were constantly bringing out body parts. Virtually none of the ancient liturgical language needed changing; yet the eucharistic worship itself was instantly charged with shock and grief as it received the self-offerings of workers who came to commune, some of them literally carrying pieces of human beings to be blessed. And then the Eucharist gave back what it had received, infused with the presence of the Holy Comforter.

An altogether different tone prevails in some new forms of the Eucharist that a South Bronx parish has chosen to celebrate out of doors in its neighborhood, rather than within its church walls. These are the now famous "hip-hop masses" sponsored by Trinity Church in the Morrisania section of the Bronx. Offered mainly for the youth of the neighborhood on Friday evenings, they take place right on the street in the rapper idiom that originated a few decades ago in this very locale. Rector Timothy Holder first came up with the idea for these Eucharists, but he quickly found support from Episcopal Bishop Catherine Roskam and Fr. Lyndon Harris. Clergy and lay leaders representing Roman Catholic, Lutheran, and other Protestant churches have also joined the movement. Vigorous singing, rapper sessions, and dancing soon became the hallmarks of the masses. Reporting on their development, Becky Garrison writes:

= Service projects at shelter in Harford County

The *Master Missal* [order of service], written, adapted, and performed by Trinity's congregation members and others from the community, translated portions of the *Book of Common Prayer* into the language of hip-hop. Co-Dance Captain Lamont, 20, from St. Paul's Church in the Bronx, wrote a *Pontifical Hip-Hop Blessing* for the services. . . . Vicar Bishop Don Taylor of the Episcopal Diocese of New York delivered the first of those blessings at a program where 100 children danced in the streets, and residents from 22 neighboring highrises surveyed the vibrant scene from their windows. . . . An early July Mass featured [Bishop] Roskam [and] New York Assemblyman Ruben Diaz, Jr.[24]

The mass in July honored some of those regarded by many as the founders of hip-hop. Kurtis Blow, Cool Clyde, Lightnin' Lance, and Jeanette Otis were all on hand for the celebration.

Here we see bold and enthusiastic efforts being made by a congregation to welcome popular culture into the ritual space of the Lord's Table. The gifts of the neighborhood are honored and received with thanksgiving. They become part of the Eucharist. But at the same time the sacrament retains its distinctive power, using its new form to proclaim the ancient gospel message of Jesus crucified and risen. Here is mission writ large, and it's not confined to the Bronx. Toward the end of her article, Garrison notes that officials at a boys' detention center just outside Richmond, Virginia, called to ask that a version of the Trinity Mass be celebrated there. Subsequent news releases indicate that the popularity of the masses continues to grow.

One last story of how the Eucharist centers our meals by attraction comes from Craig Blomberg, a well known evangelical scholar teaching at Denver Seminary. Blomberg's recent book, *Contagious Holiness: Jesus' Meals with Sinners*, offers persuasive arguments for including the many stories of Jesus' encounters with people at table in the earliest layers of the gospel tradition. He devotes the last chapter of his book to reflections on how contemporary Christian meals might reach their full potential as occasions for meeting Jesus. Building on data from the New Testament, he encourages his readers to hold frequent celebrations of the Lord's Supper, especially when they can

Imagining Caroline Center hosting a/ serving/selling a restaurant meal.

be introduced by agape meals. As an example, he cites a service he recently attended at his Baptist church in suburban Denver. The worship took place toward the end of an elders' meeting where some church members were just completing their term of office and others were coming on board to take their places. He writes:

> We shared a meal, discussed our business, and then gave the elements of Communion, one person at a time, to the person next to us. As we proceeded around the circle, each elder prayed out loud for the one sitting to his left to whom he had given the bread and wine, while also laying hands on him.[25]

There was nothing revolutionary about this eucharistic practice, but unlike so many of our liturgies today it intentionally allowed time and space for a guidance by the Spirit that expressed itself through impromptu prayers. My own experience has been that an unusual degree of openness to the Spirit prevails in business meetings when people know they're to be followed by a Eucharist. It's as if the liturgy reaches back to embrace our efforts, offering us communion with one another in Christ even as we struggle to negotiate our budgets and make our deals. At the same time we also sense that what we're doing and saying at the meeting will shortly become part of our "living sacrifice" at the Eucharist. And this consciousness affects our behavior in the debating of hard issues. It may well be that an awareness of God's presence in our meetings tends to peak when we do our business after a sit-down meal and before the Eucharist, as in the situation narrated by Blomberg. I suspect that exactly this sequence occurred in churches of the New Testament era.

Next Steps

As we end this chapter and move into a final one, it pays to reflect once again on how best to comprehend the rich interplay between our Eucharists and the other meals taking place in our congregations. We can summarize our conclusions by saying that the Eucharist reaches out to make other church-related meals more like itself. Yet those same meals present themselves at the Sunday Eucharist as part of our

Agape Meal → Eucharist

congregational self-offering, which means that we may find ourselves thinking about this formal ritual more and more in terms of a real banquet, with food and drink shared around a table. Some of us will be moved (have been moved!) to experiment with actually celebrating the Eucharist that way. For most congregations, initiating such changes within the chief Sunday service wouldn't be an easy or judicious way to go. But mid-week services, prayer breakfasts, and retreats offer plenty of opportunities for alternative liturgies.

No matter how the centrifugal-centripetal motion of the Eucharist plays itself out in our particular congregations, we can be sure that God the Holy Trinity is at work. And so are we, with our Spirit-led gifts and tasks. In fact, we've found striking examples of how meal networks in real churches can draw people more deeply into the *Missio Dei*.

Because all of the church-related meals we've looked at, including the Eucharist, engage our entire personhood with their power to nurture and challenge our outreach activities, we've made a case for using the term "soul banquets" to describe them. But now, toward the end of our study, I think we have to offer a fuller commentary on our chosen term. One big question that keeps coming up for me is how our distinctively Christian soul banquets can best connect with the rest of humanity's meals. What agendas (if any) should we Christians be following on those occasions when we take part in the meal rituals of other religions, or in the far more numerous gatherings at table these days that all participants would think of as non-religious? Can't these meals become soul banquets on their own, without intervention by Christians? This is obviously a huge issue, and I make no claim to resolving it in the current volume. Yet I think we can at least begin to develop some guidelines for Christian practices at the mixed meals of our multicultural age. In fact, I believe that the Bible itself, supplemented by personal accounts from believers who've put in a lot of time on the "frontiers of hospitality,"[26] will provide more help with our issue than many us expect. To that help we now turn.

New Testament Hospitality book

CHAPTER SIX

Table of Jesus, Feast of God

I n his gospel and Acts of the Apostles, Luke gives more attention to the details of what we've termed the mission-meal synergy than any other biblical author.[1] Yet it seems to me that just one key phrase from the Third Gospel serves to crystallize nearly all Luke's views on meals and mission, while at the same time leaping across the millennia to address our twenty-first century world. The phrase turns up in Luke's narration of the Last Supper, where he first records the familiar bread and cup words of Jesus but then adds this declaration of the Lord to his disciples:

> You are those who have stood by me in my trials; and I confer on you, just as my Father has conferred on me, a kingdom, so that you may eat and drink at my table in my kingdom . . . (Luke 22:28–30; compare Matt 19:28).

"At my table in my kingdom." Here is a shimmering little diamond, six words unique to Luke's gospel. But what sort of kingdom and table is Jesus talking about? How do the two relate to each other? When and where do they occur? Who's in and who's out, and on what terms?

Voices from Scripture

Of course scholars debate these questions endlessly. My own study of Luke-Acts over the years has led me to agree with Swedish interpreter Jacob Jervell that in Luke's view Jesus looks forward here to a reigning power that he will assume right after the resurrection, a power first disclosed when he pours out the Holy Spirit on his followers at Pentecost (Acts 2:30–33). Luke's thinking on this matter is very much like Paul's picture of Jesus reigning as Viceroy of God's kingdom in the time between the resurrection and the *parousia* or second coming (1 Cor 15:24–25). Luke further understands Jesus' prophecy at the Last Supper to mean that his Spirit-filled disciples will share his reign within a renewed Israel (Luke 22:30).[2] Like Jesus, they will "rule" only to the extent that they become servant leaders—indeed, servant leaders who tend to the feeding of dinner guests. We read that "a dispute also arose among them as to which of them was to be regarded as the greatest. But he said to them . . . 'For who is greater, the one who is at the table or the one who serves? Is it not the one at the table? But I am with you as one who serves'" (Luke 22:24–27). Here, in a not so subtle way, Jesus tells his followers: "Go and do thou likewise."

Why does Jesus choose table imagery to symbolize not only his own kingdom authority but also that of his disciples? The best answer, I think, is one that Luke gives us indirectly throughout the narrative of his gospel and Acts, namely, that Jesus and the Spirit are most regularly present to reveal God's kingdom *at meals*. In Acts, many of these table settings are distinctively Christian events because all the diners proclaim or celebrate Jesus' messiahship (e.g., Acts 2:42–47; 9:17–19; 16:14–16, 30–34). On other occasions, however, both in the ministry of Jesus and the stories of Acts, this isn't the case. Instead, we find "mixed meals," where some participants have committed themselves to Jesus (by discipleship and/or baptism), while others haven't.[3] Given the unique wording of Jesus' Last Supper prophecy in Luke, it seems most likely that he considers both categories of meals to be the Messiah's table. A bold stance of this kind follows naturally from Luke's belief that Jesus is Lord of the cosmos (Luke 1:10–11; Acts 2:34–36; 17:30–31) and that wherever his people show up at meals, he is present as the true host, whether or not all diners acknowledge him.

To some readers, Luke's position might seem to be a kind of religious imperialism, a blind certainty about one's faith that always wants to impose ideological language on ordinary conversation at mixed meals, always pushes for the conversion of those who don't yet believe. I want to suggest, however, that precisely because of Luke's strong convictions about God, Jesus, and the Holy Spirit, he takes a more sophisticated view of what actually happens at meals than the "imperialism" hypothesis permits. For one thing, Luke never forgets that Jesus' own inclusive meal practice resulted in just a few calls to discipleship (conversions). In the gospel stories most people who dined with Jesus did not drop everything to follow him.[4]

Furthermore, Luke shows evidence of using a meal prophecy found in Isaiah that does not distinguish between converted and non-converted guests. According to this vision

> the Lord of hosts will make for all peoples a feast of rich food, a feast of well-aged wines, of rich food filled with marrow, of well-aged wines strained clear. And he will destroy on this mountain the shroud that is cast over all peoples, the sheet that is spread over all nations; he will swallow up death forever. Then the Lord God will wipe away the tears from all faces and the disgrace of his people he will take away from all the earth (Isa 25:6–8).

The key phrases here are "all peoples," "all nations," and "all faces." As an avid student of the scriptures, Luke surely recognized that Isaiah's inclusive picture of God's reign on earth at the end of conventional history stood behind Jesus' famous prediction that "people will come from east and west, from north and south [i.e., from all nations] and will eat in the kingdom of God" (Luke 13:29; see also Matt 8:11). Consequently, Luke would have understood as well how the same prophecy served to inspire Jesus' distinctive practice of dining with marginal people. For the evangelist, it was clear that Jesus intended to offer a foretaste of God's kingdom banquet in his ministry, and that everyone was invited (Luke 7:31–35; Matt 11:16–18).[5]

Here, for our purposes, is the crucial point. Luke knows both the table of Jesus and the feast of God and considers them altogether compatible. The feast of God is the end-time celebration on earth of God's final triumph over evil. "All peoples" will take part in that great meal. The table of Jesus, on the other hand, signifies all eating and drinking by means of which God's kingdom feast enters into human life now through the direct influence of Jesus and the Spirit (see, for example,

Luke 10:8–9 and Acts 10:34–11:3). Such meals take place not only in Christian communities but also at their outer edges and even beyond them. For Luke, what makes a post-resurrection meal into the table of Jesus is the presence of the Risen One as recognized by at least one person. The table of Jesus has a fluid, unfinished quality. Surprises are the order of the day, as the Emmaus story makes clear (Luke 24:28–35).

Obviously, Luke doesn't answer every question we might want to pose about how the feast and the table interact, but we can infer a few things about this mysterious relationship. For example, we can see that the feast and the table belong together in one force field. They don't work at cross purposes. Moreover, we can tell from Luke's meal narratives that there's a lively cooperation between us and God taking place, though when we try to describe what's happening in terms of cause and effect, we inevitably find those terms inadequate. On the one hand, we can affirm that God's feast, which transcends ordinary space and time, reaches into our present life to transform it. That is, the kingdom comes and the *Missio Dei* moves forward in our meals because God takes the initiative (see Acts 10–11). On the other hand, we know that we ourselves must act, making our unique contributions to the missionary expansion of God's kingdom (Acts 10:19–20, 34–44).

As disciples of Jesus, as people "in Christ," we learn to share his enthusiasm about meals, and so we set our tables with high hopes. Both as hosts and as guests, we look for Jesus' presence and the gifts of the Holy Spirit, expecting that precisely at mixed meals the Spirit will help us to serve and speak words appropriate to the occasion—or no words at all. But this second option should be less frequent, for if we typically fail to express our faith in God's activity at the table and opt only for superficial talk so as not to offend anyone, we'll be restricting our sister and brother diners to short rations. We might even be starving our companions by ignoring their deepest hungers. Here the spiritual gifts of discernment and prophecy will come into play.

Three of the last meal stories in Acts offer insights into how the table of Jesus and the feast of God work together. In the first of the three, Luke narrates Paul's journey by ship to Rome as a prisoner (Acts 27:1–44). Paul is probably chained to a Roman soldier, but apparently he's accompanied and aided by one or two believers who are not prisoners.[6] The rest of the 276 passengers, crew members, and military personnel aboard the large grain ship are assumed by Luke not to be disciples of Jesus. The ship runs into a huge storm that lasts for many days, with the result that most travelers begin to fear for their lives and cease to eat. Paul, however, announces that he has seen a vision in which an angel from God promises him that no one on board will die (Acts 27:23–26).

By itself, the apostle's message doesn't suffice to calm the spirits of the passengers and crew. The storm continues, and people grow even more terrified as the ship seems about to break up on some rocks that have come into view (Acts 27:27–32). But now Paul acts decisively—whether on his own initiative or with some direct guidance from the Spirit we are not told. Here is Luke's description of the critical moment:

> Just before daybreak, Paul urged all of [the people] to take some food, saying, "Today is the fourteenth day that you have been in suspense and remaining without food, having eaten nothing. Therefore I urge you to take some food, for it will help you survive; for none of you will lose a hair from your heads." After he had said this, he took bread; and giving thanks to God in the presence of all, he broke it and began to eat. Then all of them were encouraged and took food for themselves. (We were in all two hundred seventy-six persons in the ship). After they had satisfied their hunger, they lightened the ship by throwing the wheat into the sea (Acts 27: 33–38).

Luke's account ends with the great vessel running aground on a beach and breaking into pieces—but with no loss of life whatsoever (Acts 27:39–44).

Luke obviously delights in the fact that Paul's prophecy has come true. Equally important for him, however, is the depiction of a "secular" eucharist and its salutary consequences. Commentator C. K. Barrett describes Paul's breaking of the bread in this story as follows: "As far as the language goes, this is more 'eucharistic' than any other passage in Acts. . . . The coincidence in language with that of the Last Supper cannot be missed and can hardly be accidental."[7] Although we find no words of institution in Acts 27 and Jesus' name does not occur at any point in the episode, Barrett's observation seems correct. Luke's readers would surely have noted the connection between Paul's actions and those of Jesus on the night of his arrest. Indeed, the readers of Acts have already learned that the whole reason for Paul's captivity and his subsequent trip to Rome as a prisoner is the charge brought against him that his preaching about Jesus has incited a riot in Jerusalem (Acts 22:1–26:32). Presumably a number of the apostle's shipmates also know something about this charge. It's clear, I think, that for Luke the meal at sea he chooses to narrate is the table of Jesus.

At the same time, however, Luke understands Paul's breaking of bread as an act of Divine Providence through which God reaches out to "all peoples," welcoming them to a foretaste of the feast at the kingdom's final coming. No commitment to Jesus is required. In Paul's vision the angel tells him: "God has granted safety to all those who are sailing with you" (Acts 27:24). But the people themselves cannot believe this good news until they partake of consecrated bread with the apostle, who assures them that it will help them survive [literally: "will be for your salvation"] (Acts 27:34).

How shall we summarize what Luke is telling his contemporaries (and us) in his story of Paul's shipboard meal? If we paraphrase Luke's words, the message might come out something like this:

Dear friends, as I bring my account of the church's early days to a close, I want you to feel yourselves more and more involved in the missionary action I am describing.[8] Paul's breaking of bread on the stormy sea is a paradigm for us all. Maybe things won't be so dramatic for us—but maybe they will. In any event, we'll have plenty of opportunities to eat at Jesus' table with people who don't share our faith. Expect miracles, because God is even now reaching out to all nations to seat them at the kingdom banquet. Jesus and the Spirit are with us at our meals to bring that kingdom close. Practice their presence as you eat, and you too will find yourselves hosting "secular" eucharists. Don't worry about making converts. That's God's business. Our vocation is witnessing to God's salvation as we experience it, and always with thanksgiving.

Do these words approximate Luke's true intentions? A look at two more meals stories, both in the last chapter of Acts, will show that they probably do.

The first of these is best understood as a narrative of general hospitality, with meals included. In it Luke tells how the "leading man" of Malta, one Publius, welcomed all the survivors of the shipwreck to his home for a period of three days (Acts 28:7). We can presuppose that common meals took place.[9] During this stay Paul learns—perhaps, but not necessarily at table—that the father of his host lies ill with fever and dysentery. Here is Luke's account of what happens next:

> Paul visited him and cured him by praying and putting his hands on him. After this happened, the rest of the people on the island who had diseases also came and were cured. They bestowed many honors on us, and when we were about to sail [a new ship having been commandeered], they put on board all the provisions we needed (Acts 28:8–10)

In effect, Paul takes on the role of host at the home of Publius. His prayer for healing most likely invokes the name of Jesus (see Acts 3:1–8; 4:7–10, 29–30; 8:4–8; 9:19, 34), so we can think of the whole three day event as Jesus' table. Yet, as far as we know, conversions to faith in Jesus do not follow the healings. Luke probably means for us to interpret them as free blessings from God to "all peoples." They are signs of the kingdom feast drawing near (as in Luke 10:8–9) and do not require a specific faith response.

The very last meal story in Acts is also the conclusion of Acts—a fact worth noting. As in the Publius narrative, we have to use our imaginations a little to see the table setting; but there's strong linguistic evidence that Luke wants us to do exactly that. The scene is an apartment in Rome, where Paul the prisoner—in all likelihood still chained to a soldier-guard[10]—has been allowed to stay while awaiting his trial before the emperor. Luke says of the apostle that "He lived there [in his lodging] two whole years at his own expense and welcomed all who came to him, proclaiming the kingdom of God and teaching about the Lord Jesus Christ with all boldness and without hindrance" (Acts 28:30–31).

To get the right perspective on the cameo Luke is painting here, we need to unpack the word "welcomed." In Greek it's *apedecheto*, which could mean simply "greet" in a warm and friendly manner. But in

Luke 9:10–11 we find the same verb used to describe what Jesus does just prior to feeding the five thousand. The story goes as follows: "He took [the disciples] with him and withdrew privately to a city called Bethsaida. When the crowds found out about it, they followed him, and he welcomed them (*apodexomenos autous*) and spoke to them about the kingdom of God and healed those who needed to be cured." Then, toward the end of the day, Jesus multiplied the loaves and fishes for the crowd to eat (Luke 9:12–17). This feeding miracle occurs in all four canonical gospels, but it's noteworthy that only Luke introduces it with a reference to Jesus' gesture of welcoming and talk about the kingdom (Matthew joins Luke in mentioning healings). For the third evangelist this particular welcoming, which expands into teaching and healing, becomes a natural prelude to a miraculous common meal.

It seems quite likely that in Acts 28:30–31 Luke wants his readers to see Paul imitating his Lord's welcoming. Like Jesus, he combines gospel proclamation with the offering of a meal, albeit an everyday one.[11] If this is an accurate reading of the text, it follows that the apostle has once again taken up the role of host at the table of Jesus. "All who came to him" in his apartment probably means both Jews and Gentiles. In addition, we must imagine Paul's soldier-guard standing by or seated, perhaps eating with him and his guests. He could well be the same guard who accompanied Paul throughout the stormy voyage and its aftermath on Malta. For Luke, the meals offered by Paul draw "all sorts and conditions" to the table; moreover, they come laden with traditions about other meals in which believers have participated. No conversions are reported, but clearly seeds are being planted and the *Missio Dei* is moving forward. We can paraphrase Luke's final message to his readers this way: "You too can do something like this at the tables you set or attend."

How do Luke's thoughts about the missionary potential of mixed meals translate into our own church life? If we want to retain his terminology, we could say that in our meals too the table of Jesus intersects with, interacts with, gives to and receives from the feast of God. As in the pluralistic settings sketched by Luke, so also in our own mixed meals, we may invoke Jesus' name explicitly, or we may witness to it indirectly through other words and actions. In either case, the end-time feast of God's kingdom will be constantly reaching into our table communion to sanctify it and all those who join it. Whenever we take our Christian identity seriously at meals, we're presented with extraordinary opportunities for entering more deeply into God's saving plan. Our cooperation with the kingdom coming at table may or may not result in conversions. That is God's business.

Voices from the Frontiers

In a recent essay Archbishop Rowan Williams makes a case for Christian identity and action in a pluralistic world that's surprisingly compatible with Luke's focus on meals.[12] Williams uses the metaphor of "place" to describe who Christians are and what we are called to do as we increasingly mingle with cultures and faith traditions that are unfamiliar to us. He writes: "Christian identity is to belong in a place that Jesus defines for us. By living [there], we come in some degree to share his identity, to bear his name and to be in the same relationships he has with God and with the world."[13] Williams understands this place to be "exclusive" because all of us occupying it begin from a scripturally defined sense of our life in Christ. Not everyone has that faith consciousness. But seen from another perspective, our home base as disciples of Jesus is "inclusive" because "the place of Jesus is open to all who want to see what Christians see and to become what Christians are becoming. And no Christian believer has in his or her possession some kind of map of where exactly the boundaries of that place are to be fixed, or a key to lock others out or in."[14]

What would happen if we concretized the "place" metaphor that Williams employs by understanding it in terms of meals? These events, we have been insisting, are some of the most regular settings in our Christian life where our identity shows up in the presence of others. We surely don't own the table of Jesus or the feast of God. Nor, as Williams says, do we fix their exact boundaries. The Spirit blows where it wills, and often outside of church structures. Yet our faith, formed by the Old and New Testaments, constantly urges us to seek out meals as a wellspring for mission. Sometimes we host these events; sometimes we participate as guests. Often we move back and forth from one role to the other in the course of a single meal. Increasingly these days we dine in settings defined by those whose customs and beliefs we find strange. Often we'll feel that we have less control over the mixed meals we attend than the confident Paul of Acts 27–28. Yet we come to all of them enriched by the gift of our place in Christ, and that is enough.

At one point in his essay Williams makes a direct connection between our Christian place and the Eucharist. He puts it this way:

> I believe that our emphasis should not be on possessing a system [of beliefs and practices] in which all questions are answered, but precisely on witness to the place and the identity that we have been invited to live in. We are to show what we see, to reproduce the life of God as it has been delivered to us by the anointed . . . When Christians pray the eucharistic prayer, they take the place of Jesus, both as he prays to the Father and as he offers welcome to the world at his table. The Eucharist is the celebration of the God who keeps promises and whose hospitality is always to be trusted.[15]

To this I say "Amen," and I think Luke would, too. Yet I'd want to add that church-based Eucharists aren't the only tables at which our Christian place reveals itself as God's welcome to the world.

Karen Olson knows a lot about those other meals. Karen is the founder (in 1986) of the Interfaith Hospitality Network, through which more than a hundred thousand volunteers all across the country work with churches and synagogues to provide homeless guests with safe and comfortable quarters, meals, and services. Clearly, IHN is about much more than meals, but I have to think that Karen's bringing it to birth followed directly from an encounter with the feast of God. Calvin Ross, who interviewed her, tells this story:

> On an impulse in 1981, a business commuter bought a sandwich for an elderly, homeless woman whom she had often passed on her route in New York City. "I just wanted to drop that sandwich and move on," Karen Olson remembers, "but she grabbed my hand and we talked for several minutes. I realized that she was hungry not only for food but even more for human warmth and compassion."

Serving that sandwich changed the course of Karen's life. She got to know that woman . . . and many other homeless New Yorkers. Karen and her two sons began delivering sandwiches to homeless people in the Port Authority Bus Terminal on Sunday evenings. In listening to their life stories, the Olsons learned that homelessness is more than houselessness. . . . To be homeless is often to experience the profound loss of family and friends, and the support system that connects most of us to a stable life.

Karen learned that even in her home community of Union City, New Jersey, there were hundreds of homeless people, including many families . . . [she] turned to the religious community for help.[16]

Over the next few months several planning meetings took place, and under Karen's direction religious groups of various kinds began to pool their resources. She recalls that

Ten churches and one synagogue came forward to provide hospitality space within their buildings, the local YMCA agreed to provide showers and a room for the families during the day, a car dealer discounted a van, and a foundation provided a grant for the rest. On October 27, 1986, the first Interfaith Hospitality Network opened its doors.[17]

Less than two years later, when similar groups formed elsewhere in New Jersey and congregations outside the state sought guidance for providing comprehensive service to homeless people, the National Interfaith Hospitality Network was formed. It has since changed its name to Family Promise.

Calvin Ross and others who have chronicled the organization's growth over the past decade find it noteworthy that most of those who serve in it and are served by it experience a strange transcendence pervading their activities.[18] People use different words to describe this feeling but agree that it often surfaces at the regular family dinners where relationships between sponsoring congregations and their guests first take shape and then mature as members and guests repeatedly serve one another at the table. Readers may remember my account of one such IHN dinner at St. Mark's Church in Cheyenne, Wyoming (see Chapter Three).

Here I think that we may dare to speak once again of God's feast entering our lives, and in such a way that no particular religious group can make claims about controlling it. Although most communities who support the IHN are Christian in background, and their meals exhibit this faith commitment, other Network groups originate in synagogues and non-sectarian organizations like the YM/YWCA. We Christians will naturally want to affirm our identity as servants at the table of Jesus whenever we host meals for those in need. Our calling requires an intentional witness to our convictions. But on many occasions we'll also have the sense of being caught up into a larger Mission, a mystery that we ought not label prematurely with our in-house theological language. When this happens, we'll speak humbly, aware that like other religious people we have much to learn about the ways of God. Indeed, our faith tells us that something as basic as getting to know Christ is a life-long process (Phil 3:10–15).

The day to day aspects of our journey as disciples were probably on Miriam Therese Winter's mind when she wrote:

> Sacramental meals, sacramental moments permeate our lives, whether or not we know it. To know is to be receptive to the force of each meal's blessings and to be nurtured by the memory of that moment or that meal . . . It is good to come together for a meal with those who are close to us. It is also essential to invite to our table those beyond our inner circle, if we would change the dynamic of a xenophobic world. The meals we share with family and friends, with the passerby, with strangers, are like the table fellowship of Jesus.[19]

I'd go just one step further, affirming with Luke that such gatherings for food and drink *are* a form of table fellowship with Jesus.

These days, the growing phenomenon of interfaith meals may open up special opportunities for the maturing of our faith and our mission. What spiritual gifts, for example, might we give and receive as we sit with our Jewish neighbors at Passover seders or Sabbath eve dinners? What might we learn and teach about God's loving purposes for humankind when we join Muslim friends in the feasting that marks the end of Ramadan? And what will happen at the burgeoning number of mixed meals where diverse faith communities and those of no faith find themselves engaged in a common task, yet with no one group acting as host? The answers to these questions aren't easy to envision, but for me simply posing them is an exciting prospect. Two things I'm pretty certain about. One is that the meals where such questions arise will turn out to be Soul Banquets. The other is that from those tables the *Missio Dei* will move forward with new power.

Notes

Introduction

1. For an overview of Jesus' acts and sayings as they relate to meals, see my *New Testament Hospitality: Partnership with Strangers as Promise and Mission* (Eugene, Ore.: Wipf and Stock Publishers, 2001; originally published in 1985), 15–51.

2. Ibid., 124–148, and John Koenig, *The Feast of the World's Redemption: Eucharistic Origins and Christian Mission* (Harrisburg, Pa.: Trinity Press International, 2000), 215–259.

3. Brian McLaren, *A Generous Orthodoxy* (Grand Rapids: Zondervan, 2004), 105.

4. Ibid., 107–8.

5. Ibid., 113.

6. David Bosch, *Transforming Mission: Paradigm Shifts in Theology of Mission* (Maryknoll, N.Y.: Orbis, 2004; originally published in 1992), 10.

Chapter One

1. No author named, "Notes from Ground Zero," *Via Media*, 1 (2002): 4.

2. John Koenig, *New Testament Hospitality: Partnership with Strangers as Promise and Mission* (Eugene, Ore: Wipf and Stock Publishers, 2001), 15–16.

3. Tessa Rajak, *The Jewish Dialogue with Greece and Rome: Studies in Cultural and Social Interaction* (Boston: Brill Academic Publishers, 1999), 10–11.

4. Miriam Therese Winter, *eucharist with a small "e"* (Maryknoll, N.Y.: Orbis Books, 2005), 90–91.

5. John Koenig, *The Feast of the World's Redemption: Eucharistic Origins and the Christian Mission* (Harrisburg, Pa.: Trinity Press International, 2000), 41–44.

6. Mortimer Arias, "Centripetal Mission or Evangelization by Hospitality," *Missiology: An International Review* 10 (1983): 69–81.

7. Roger W. Gehring, *House Church and Mission: The Importance of Household Structures in Early Christianity* (Peabody, Mass.: Hendrickson Publishers, Inc., 2004), 91, 295.

8. Luke Timothy Johnson, *Religious Experience in Earliest Christianity* (Minneapolis: Fortress Press, 1998), 137–179.

9. Koenig, *Feast of the World's Redemption*, 180.

10. W. D. Davies-Allison, Dale C. Allison, Jr., *A Critical and Exegetical Commentary on the Gospel According to Saint Matthew (International Critical Commentary) Vol. 2* (Edinburgh: T. & T. Clark Publishers, Ltd., 1989), 790.

11. Paul Wilkes, *Excellent Catholic Parishes: The Guide to Best Places and Practices* (Mahwah, N.J.: Paulist Press, 2001), 179.

12. Craig L. Blomberg, *Contagious Holiness: Jesus' Meals With Sinners* (Downers Grove, Ill.: InterVarsity Press, 2005), 176.

13. Katie Zezima, "Religion Journal; Over Cocktails, a Relaxed Give and Take on Catholicism," *New York Times* (Nov. 12, 2005): A16.

14. Daniel Sack, *Whitebread Protestants: Food and Religion in American Culture* (New York: Palgrave, 2001), 62.

15. John Navone, "The Lukan Banquet Community," *Bible Today* 51 (1970): 155–161.

16. Dennis E. Smith, *From Symposium to Eucharist: The Banquet in the Early Christian World* (Minneapolis: Augsburg Fortress, 2003).

17. Koenig, *Feast of the World's Redemption*, 87–126, 133–138.

18. Jacob Jervell, *Luke and the People of God: A New Look at Luke-Acts* (Minneapolis: Augsburg Publishing House, 1972), 75–112.

19. Koenig, *New Testament Hospitality* 85–123.

Chapter Two

1. Gerhard Friedrich, ed; vol IX of *Theological Dictionary of the New Testament*, trans. Geoffrey W. Bromiley (Grand Rapids, Mich.: William B. Eerdmans Publishing Company, 1974), 402–406.

2. Max Weber, *The Sociology of Religion*, trans. Ephraim Fischoff (Boston: Beacon Press, 1991).

3. One liturgical scholar, Paul Bradshaw, thinks that the very earliest eucharistic prayers were probably "short acclamations and/or invocations that varied from service to service." Such prayers can easily be understood as Spirit-led. Paul F. Bradshaw, *The Search for the Origins of Christian Worship: Sources and Methods for the Study of Early Liturgy* (New York: Oxford University Press, 2002), 141.

4. For a discussion of how so-called "natural" processes, talents, and events can be experienced as charismatic, see: John Koenig, *Charismata: God's Gifts for God's People* (Philadelphia: The Westminster Press, 1978), 124–127.

5. Any good commentary on Romans will help us with this issue. I recommend James D. G. Dunn, *Romans 9–16*, Word Biblical Commentary Vol. 38b (Dallas: Word Books, 1988).

6. John Koenig, *The Feast of the World's Redemption: Eucharistic Origins and the Christian Mission* (Harrisburg, Pa.: Trinity Press International, 2000), 102–126. See also 127–164, 165–214.

7. Andrew P. McGowan, "Is There a Liturgical Text in this Gospel?" *Journal of Biblical Literature* 116 (1999): 73–87.

8. Robert Banks, *Going to Church in the First Century: An Eyewitness Account* (Auburn, Me.: Christian Books Publishing House, 1990), 38–46.

9. Koenig, *Feast of the World's Redemption* 133–138.

10. Dennis E. Smith, *From Symposium to Eucharist* (Minneapolis: Fortress Press, 2003), 173–218.

11. John Koenig, *New Testament Hospitality: Partnership with Strangers as Promise and Mission* (Eugene, Ore: Wipf and Stock Publishers, 2001), 69.

12. Elizabeth O'Connor, *The Eighth Day of Creation: Gifts and Creativity* (Waco, Texas: Word Books, 1971), 25.

13. Elizabeth O'Connor, *The New Community: A Portrait of Life Together in Words and Pictures* (New York: Harper & Row, 1976), 27–28.

14. Ibid., 30.

15. Ibid., 53.

16. Paul Wilkes, *Excellent Protestant Congregations: The Guide to Best Places and Practices* (Louisville: Westminster John Knox Press, 2001) 21–38, 197–259 and *Excellent Catholic Parishes* (Mahwah, N.J.: Paulist Press, 2001), 195–255.

17. Ben Campbell Johnson and Glenn McDonald, *Imagining a Church in the Spirit: A Task for Mainline Congregations* (Grand Rapids, Mich.: William B. Eerdmans Publishing Company, 1999), 53.

18. Ibid., 9, 28.

19. Ibid., 74.

20. Ibid., 82–84.

21. The cathedral's website notes that: "Trinity's Sudanese Ministry is an ecumenical ministry shared with the Roman Catholic Church involving the nearly 60 Sudanese college-age refugees often referred to as the Lost Boys of Sudan. The Trinity community includes many active members and families who are Sudanese. Their worship traditions and language add a wonderful dimension to many Sunday services." (See: http://www.trinitysj.org/ministries/sudanese.html.)

Chapter Three

1. James D. G. Dunn, *Romans 9–16*, Word Biblical Commentary Vol. 38b (Dallas: Word Books, 1988), 823.

2. Alexander Schmemann, *For the Life of the World* (Crestwood, N.Y.: St. Vladimir's Seminary Press, 1998), 44.

3. This term originated with the Italian journalist Carlo Petrini. In his book *Slow Food*, he makes the case for eating as a leisurely group activity and sees food preparation as part of this. Petrini criticizes our American fixation with "fast food," where the quick refueling of individuals is a priority. See Carlo Petrini, *Slow Food: The Case for Taste*, trans. William McCuaig (New York: Columbia University Press, 1994).

4. Roger W. Gehring, *House Church and Mission: The Importance of Household Structures in Early Christianity* (Peabody, Mass.: Hendrickson Publishers, Inc., 2004), 141.

5. Richard Giles, *Re-Pitching the Tent: Re-Ordering the Church Building for Worship and Mission*, 2nd edition (Collegeville, Minn.: Liturgical Press, 2004), 130.

6. Robin Jensen, *Face to Face: Portraits of the Divine in Early Christianity* (Minneapolis: Fortress Press, 2005).

7. Princeton is Buechner's real-life alma mater.

8. Frederick Buechner, *Love Feast* (New York: Atheneum, 1974), 240. See also 93, 192, 241–243.

9. More information about hospitality networks in North America can be found in Calvin W. Ross, *Hosting the Unknown: Making Room in the House of God for Homeless Families* (Johnson City, Tenn.: 2005).

10. Elizabeth Rankin Geitz, *Entertaining Angels: Hospitality Programs for the Caring Church* (Harrisburg, Pa.: Morehouse Publishing, 1993), 86.

11. Henri J. M. Nouwen, *Reaching Out: The Three Movements of the Spiritual Life* (Garden City, N.Y.: Doubleday & Company, Inc., 1975), 50.

12. Elizabeth Maxwell and Susan Shapiro, ed., *Food for the Soul: Selections from the Holy Apostles Soup Kitchen Writers' Workshop* (New York: Church Publishing Inc., 2004), xii.

13. Ibid., xi, xv.

14. Ibid., xv.

15. Ibid., xviii.

16. Russell Chandler, *Feeding the Flock: Restaurants and Churches You'd Stand in Line For* (Herndon, Va.: The Alban Institute, 1998).

17. Ibid., 8.

18. Two basic textbooks in this important field are Murray Bowen, *Family Therapy in Clinical Practice* (Northvale, N.J.: Jason Aronson, 1978) and Edwin H. Friedman, *Family Process in Church and Synagogue*, (New York: Guilford Press, 1983).

Chapter Four

1. For more on this, see Lawrence A. Hoffman, *The Art of Public Prayer: Not for Clergy Only*, Washington, D.C.: The Pastoral Press, 1988) and John Koenig, *Rediscovering New Testament Prayer: Boldness and Blessing in the Name of Jesus* (Harrisburg, Pa.: Morehouse Publishing, 1998).

2. Frances Moore Lappé, *Diet for a Small Planet: 20th Anniversary Edition* (New York: Ballantine Books, 1991).

3. Daniel Sack, *Whitebread Protestants: Food and Religion in American Culture* (New York: Palgrave, 2001), 211.

4. A recent work that calls us to account for our complicity in high-profit food production systems but doesn't get stuck in moralizing platitudes is L. Shannon Jung's *Food for Life: The Spirituality and Ethics of Eating* (Minneapolis: Augsburg Fortress, 2004). See especially Jung's last chapter on "A New Vision for the Church," which beautifully accents the grace of God in our meals.

5. The full text of Herbert's poem is available on numerous websites and in *The Norton Anthology of English Literature*, 6th ed. vol. 1 (New York: W. W. Norton & Company, 1993).

6. See 2 Cor 8–9, where Paul pressures his readers to complete a collection of money by extolling the generosity of their neighbor churches in Macedonia.

7. Paul David Lawson, *Old Wine in New Skins: Centering Prayer and Systems Theory* (New York: Lantern Books, 2001). Lawson builds on extensive clinical work done by the pioneering psychotherapists Murray Bowen and Edwin Friedman.

8. See M. Basil Pennington, *Centering Prayer: Renewing an Ancient Christian Prayer Form* (Garden City, N.Y.: Doubleday & Company, Inc., 1980) and Thomas Keating, *Open Mind, Open Heart: The Contemplative Dimension of the Gospel* (New York: Continuum International Publishing Group, 1986).

9. Walter Wink, *Unmasking the Powers: The Invisible Forces that Determine Human Existence* (Philadelphia: Fortress Press, 1986).

10. Ibid., 69–86.

11. Ibid., 73–82.

12. Regarding the angels, I suspect that John saw them as celestial servants who made sure that Christ's messages were actually delivered to their intended audiences, probably through local leaders of worship assemblies. Paul has similar views on angels and prophets (see 1 Corinthians 11:10; 13:1).

13. Richard Bauckham, *The Theology of the Book of Revelation* (Cambridge, U.K.: Cambridge University, 1993), 1–17.

14. Roger W. Gehring, *House Church and Mission: The Importance of Household Structures in Early Christianity* (Peabody, Mass.: Hendrickson Publishers, Inc., 2004), 131.

15. Henri J. M. Nouwen, *With Burning Hearts: A Meditation on the Eucharistic Life* (Maryknoll, N.Y.: Orbis Books, 1994), 60.

16. David Anderson, *Breakfast Epiphanies: Finding Wonder in the Everyday* (Boston: Beacon Press, 2004), 3–4.

17. Gordon Fee, *The First Epistle to the Corinthians (The New International Commentary on the New Testament)* (Grand Rapids, Mich.: William B. Eerdmans Publishing Company, 1987), 568.

18. James D. G. Dunn, *Romans 9–16*, Word Biblical Commentary Vol. 38b (Dallas: Word Books, 1988), 150 f.

19. Ian Fisher, " Pope Rules Quietly, Quietly, but Maybe Actively," *New York Times*: November 25, 2005.

20. The material on *Babette's Feast* that follows comes from my memory of viewing the movie version on two separate occasions. One can find plot summaries, reviews, discussions of both the film and the story, and even links to recipes at www.karenblixen.com.

Chapter Five

1. Paul McPartlan, *The Eucharist Makes the Church: Henri de Lubac and John Zizioulas in Dialogue* (Edinburgh, Scotland: T&T Clark, 1993).

2. John Koenig, *The Feast of the World's Redemption: Eucharistic Origins and the Christian Mission* (Harrisburg, Pa.: Trinity Press International, 2000), 50–54.

3. Ibid., 10–14, 67–76. The range of dates presupposes Paul's conversion to faith in Jesus only a year or two after the crucifixion and his reception of the Lord's Supper tradition not long after that.

4. Ibid., 69–74.

5. Ibid., 75.

6. Ibid., 193–211.

7. William K. McElvaney, *Eating and Drinking at the Welcome Table: The Holy Supper for All People* (St. Louis: Chalice Press, 1998), xi.

8. Ibid., 14.

9. Ibid., 15.

10. John Wilson, "This Is My Body: Is There a Eucharistic Revival Afoot?." *Beliefnet*, Oct. 13, 2000, http://www.beliefnet.com/story/46/story_4688.html (accessed June 8, 2006).

11. Anecdotal evidence suggests that in some of the so-called "emerging churches," which range from auditorium-sized to very small, the Eucharist has already achieved a great deal of prominence. See: Eddie Gibbs and Ryan K Bolger, *Emerging Churches: Creating Christian Community in Postmodern Cultures* (Grand Rapids, Mich.: Baker Academic, 2005), 119–120, 225, 227, 228–229.

12. The expression "making one's communion" occurs regularly in Roman Catholic and Anglican Catholic circles. It highlights the human effort required to present ourselves at the sacrament with hope and intentionality.

13. The NRSV translation of 1 Corinthians 11:28–29 hides the fact that Paul thinks of individual persons doing this discernment within a corpo-

rate service of worship. For Paul, the service involves a full supper, where the normal posture would be sitting or reclining.

14. Owen Chadwick, *Michael Ramsey: A Life* (New York: Oxford University Press, 1990), 47. Quoted in Koenig, *Feast of the World's Redemption*, 249.

15. McElvaney, *Eating and Drinking*, 28–39.

16. Miriam Therese Winter, *eucharist with a small "e"* (Maryknoll, N.Y.: Orbis Books, 2005), 147.

17. Peter Cruchley-Jones, "A Eucharistic Understanding of Mission—A Missiological Understanding of Eucharist," in *Mission Matters*, ed. Lynne Price, Juan Sepúlveda, and Graeme Smith (Frankfurt am Main: Peter Lang Publishing Group, 1997), 100–119. Cruchley-Jones has also produced a book-length treatment of the topic entitled *Singing the Lord's Song in a Strange Land?: A Missiological Interpretation Of the Ely Pastorate Churches, Cardiff* (Frankfurt am Main: Peter Lang Publishing Group, 2001).

18. Cruchley-Jones, "Eucharistic Understanding of Mission," 115.

19. Cruchley-Jones, *Singing The Lord's Song*, 152.

20. J.G. Davies, *Worship and Mission* (London: SCM Press, 1966), 120.

21. See Koenig, *Feast of the World's Redemption*, 133–138, for the view that Romans 12 presupposes a eucharistic liturgy.

22. 1 Cor 14:1, 22–25. See also the directions for holding eucharistic meals in the early Christian document called *The Didache*. At the end of these instructions we read: "But permit the prophets to give thanks [or hold the Eucharist] as often as they wish" (10:7, Ehrman's translation). Most interpreters think this passage refers to eucharistic liturgies that are suffused with oracular speech.

23. Winter, *eucharist with a small "e,"* 123.

24. Becky Garrison, "The Word on the Streets: Hip-hop Masses Rock the Bronx," *Episcopal Life* (Sept. 2004): 10.

25. Craig L. Blomberg, *Contagious Holiness: Jesus' Meals With Sinners* (Downers Grove, Ill.: InterVarsity Press, 2005), 179.

26. This phrase is the title of the last chapter of my book *New Testament Hospitality*, 124–148. There I try to show that a good deal of our Christian welcoming (including meals) will consist of forming partnerships with "strangers," that is, people who don't necessarily share our beliefs about God, but who nevertheless want to make the world into a more hospitable place.

Chapter Six

1. For an analysis of this phenomenon, see *New Testament Hospitality*, "Guests and Hosts, Together in Mission (Luke)," 85–123.

2. J. Jervell, *Luke and the People of God: A New Look at Luke-Acts* (Minneapolis: Augsburg Publishing House, 1972), 75–112.

3. In Luke's gospel, see 5:27–32; 7:36–50; and 15:1–2, where it is assumed that not everyone present is committed to Jesus. For the same phenomenon in Acts see chapters 27 and 28.

4. This is certainly the implication of Luke 5:27–32; 14:1–14; and 15:1–2.

5. See B. Chilton, *Pure Kingdom: Jesus' Vision of God* (Grand Rapids: Wm. B. Eerdmans Pub. Co.,1996), 13, 88; and C. Blomberg, *Contagious Holiness*, 58–59, 101, 113–114.

6. Acts 27:1–2 appears to be the journal of a narrator who was present ("When it was decided that we were to set sail for Italy. . . ") and mentions another companion of Paul's named Aristarchus. Neither of these people is identified as a prisoner.

7. C. K. Barrett, *The Acts of the Apostles* (London and New York: T & T Clark, 1998) The International Critical Commentary, vol. II, 1208–1209.

8. L. C. A. Alexander offers helpful observations on how Luke draws his readers into the narrative of Acts, particularly in the book's closing chapters. See *Acts in Its Ancient Literary Context: A Classicist Looks at the Acts of the Apostles* (London and New York: T. and T. Clark, 2005), 226–229.

9. The three day rule for entertaining strangers with overnight accommodations, food, and drink was widely practiced in the ancient Mediterranean world.

10. One can imagine the two eating together on some occasions.

11. In discussing Paul's domestic arrangements in Rome, B. Rapske concludes that the apostle, though a prisoner, was most likely allowed to prepare his own meals from provisions supplied by friends. Rapske does not deal with the question of whether Acts 20:30 describes meals that Paul offered to visitors. See *The Book of Acts and Paul in Roman Custody* (Grand Rapids: Wm B. Eerdmans Publishing Co., 1994). *The Book of Acts in Its First Century Setting*, vol. 3, 237–239.

12. The essay, called "Christians Among Others: Identify Yourself," is adapted from a speech delivered by Williams at the assembly of the World

Council of Churches in Porto Alegre, Brazil. It appeared in the March 21, 2006 issue of *The Christian Century*.

13. Ibid., 29.

14. Ibid., 29.

15. Ibid., 30.

16. C. W. Ross, *Hosting the Unknown: Making Room in Houses of God for Homeless Families* (Johnson City, Tenn.: Johannine Press, 2005), 25.

17. Ibid., 26.

18. Ibid., 17–48.

19. *eucharist with a small "e,"* 125–126.

Index